Science's
Blind Spot

Science's Blind Spot

The Unseen Religion of Scientific Naturalism

Cornelius G. Hunter

Brazos Press
Grand Rapids, Michigan

Published by Brazos Press
a division of Baker Publishing Group
P.O. Box 6287, Grand Rapids, MI 49516-6287
www.brazospress.com

Printed in the United States of America

Library of Congress Cataloging-in-Publication Data

Hunter, Cornelius G.
    Science's blind spot / Cornelius G. Hunter.
      p. cm.
    Includes bibliographical references (p.   ) and index..
    ISBN 10: 1-58743-170-X (pbk.)
    ISBN 978-1-58743-170-8 (pbk.)
    1. Religion and science. 2. Naturalism—Religious aspects. I. Title.
BL240.3.H86 2007
201′.65—dc22
                                               2006029549

Contents

Preface

This book is about a centuries-old movement in science. Although this movement is tremendously important in today's world, it goes largely unnoticed. It dominates science, and its influence beyond science is far reaching, yet it remains largely unknown to both scientist and lay person alike. This movement goes unnoticed not because it is a *secret*, but because it is *pervasive*. There is no single founder, no famous scientist or philosopher to associate with the movement. There is no particular group, nor even label associated with the idea. Rather, it has been held and promoted by a variety of thinkers from a wide range of traditions.

As Alfred North Whitehead once suggested, assumptions and premises that are crucial to a movement are often deemed to be obvious and in no need of justification. These underlying assumptions are unspoken and undefended because, as Whitehead put it, "Such assumptions appear so obvious that people do not know what they are assuming because no other way of putting things has ever occurred to them."[1] Whitehead's observation well describes the subject of this book.

Scientific conclusions, which may have implications far beyond the world of science, often depend on deeply held assumptions that would be difficult to defend under close scrutiny. The consequences of this are enormous, for this movement is both profound and yet presumed—crucial and broadly influential, yet taken for granted. We need to evaluate its underlying assumptions because, in many ways, these assumptions are now dictating our thinking. Our conclusions and opinions of today have deep roots.

For this book I am indebted to many people. These include John Bloom, David Snoke, Ken Daniels, and George Murphy for their helpful comments and criticisms. I am, of course, responsible for any errors in the book.

1

What's Wrong with Science

Over the past four centuries science has made wonderful discoveries. It would be a challenge just to document all the ways that science has improved our lives. Science investigates the natural world with great success. It seems to be synonymous with knowledge and truth. Can we even question science? Can there be anything wrong with science? The answer, of course, is yes. Like all endeavors science has its weak points and challenges. It is successful, but it is not perfect. The biggest challenge that science faces stems from religion. The problem is not, as is sometimes popularly held, that religion opposes science. The problem is that religion has joined science.

Religious beliefs and traditions have had profound influences on science, more than is often understood. These influences were important in the early formational years of modern science, and they remain important today. In centuries past the church supported science in several ways. But support does not come without cost. Religious support was accompanied by religious influence, though the connection was sometimes subtle.

Tell me who paid for the scientific research, so goes the old joke, and I'll tell you the results. But there are deeper influences in science than the color of the funding money. Within scientific communities there usually are tacit understandings of what types of results are acceptable and what types are not. Ideally such understandings are merely based on existing knowledge gained the hard way—from empirically based scientific work. But too often they are based on accepted norms that are unproved and unquestioned. Research that is bought and paid for by special interest groups is obvious. Religious influences are often less obvious and more pervasive.

The message that religion has been smuggled into science is not common today. Historians take note of the many religious influences in centuries past, but that, we are told, is now all gone. Today's science is thought to be empirical and free of theological premise. It is admitted that individual scientists hold their own religious beliefs. But science itself, according to many commentators, is free of theological guide or constraint. Nothing could be further from the truth.

How We Got Here

There were many religious influences within science in centuries past. In fact, theological concerns often guided and constrained scientific ideas and thought. A variety of such concerns were raised by different thinkers at different times. This makes them both easy to see but not necessarily easy to categorize. These ideas were prevalent but complex—there was no single religious tradition, no single theological concern, no leading thinker or even school of thought at the interface between religion and science. What was the motivation for these religious ideas, how were they related, and, importantly, exactly what influence did these religious ideas have on science?

The answers to such questions are not simple, but on the other hand, they are not beyond our reach. There are strong connections between religion and science, and recurring themes are obvious. Theological premises do not merely suggest possibilities or stimulate thinking—they are at times crucial in framing scientific thought. This book traces out these connections and their effects.

We begin in chapter 2 with a survey of several common religious influences in the seventeenth through nineteenth centuries. Most of them fall into four distinct categories: greater God theology, religious rationalism and deism, the problem of evil, and theological opposition to miracles. These categories are overarching. None of them represents a single tradition or concern; rather, each arises from a family of similar concerns. And these categories do not capture the totality of religious thought impinging on science. Other concerns that we will see in later chapters include the warning against anthropomorphizing God, the God of the gaps warning, the infinite regress problem, and the intellectual necessity.

This history and framework gives helpful structure to the religion-science interface. As we shall see, these different theological traditions would circumscribe scientific activity by defining what types of solutions were, and were not, acceptable. Indeed, these theological mandates are common in the scientific literature.

There are, as it were, theological ground rules imposed on science. And although these theological concerns are varied, they all funnel toward a similar consequence. Put simply, the primary theological ground rule is that scientific explanations must be purely naturalistic. The term *naturalism* can take on different meanings when used by historians and philosophers of science. Here it is used to refer to this restriction of science to naturalistic explanations for religious reasons. I use a new term, *theological naturalism*, to clarify this and avoid ambiguity.

The term *theological naturalism* reminds us that the assumption of naturalism in science is neither a result of atheistic influence nor an empirically based scientific finding. It is a consequence of metaphysical reasoning, and the implications for science are profound. Theological naturalism provides science with well-defined universal criteria to which it conforms. Instead of merely following the data wherever it may lead, science has a framework already in place. The answer, to a certain extent, is already in place. This is a move toward rationalism and away from empiricism. The result is that science has a powerful philosophy of science, but as we shall see in chapter 3, it does not come without cost. Theological naturalism brings with it a blind spot.

Theological naturalism also has implications for how theories in science are evaluated. Theories that otherwise have significant evidential problems may gain wide acceptance if they are in accord with theological naturalism. Chapters 4, 5, and 6 examine theories in which theological naturalism is particularly important. Truth claims that empirical science could never make abound.

Chapters 7, 8, and 9 examine the situation today. The impact of theological naturalism is profound and goes beyond science. Everything from individual careers to public policy and, yes, theology is affected. For science is not seen as influenced by theological naturalism but as independently corroborating theological naturalism. For many this is a compelling convergence. Today's wisdom is that we have made profound discoveries about the world. But, in fact, these discoveries have deep connections to assumptions made centuries ago.

It may seem ironic that religious thought mandates naturalism in science. Isn't religion opposed to naturalism? This naive view arises from what is unfortunately an all-too-common shallow understanding of religion. Theologians of various stripes, today and in centuries past, have argued vigorously that nature is strictly naturalistic, and this sentiment has gripped science. As we shall see, religious thinking pervades science today, yet this is not generally understood.

Religion has damaged science, and the problem is compounded by the widespread misconception that science is mostly free of religious influence. Like a cancer that quietly destroys, religious influence has caused problems, but ignorance of the influence is the more serious problem. The relationship between religion and science can be improved, and alternative ways of doing science can be contemplated. But we first need to understand science and how it has been shaped by religion.

2

The Revolution That Wasn't

odern science is about four centuries old. The occasion of its birth was more of a change in thinking than a change in technology. It was not simply that new technologies and devices cleared the way for scientific research: there was an important philosophical shift that ushered in what we now think of as modern science. This much is understood. What is not so well understood, however, is the precise nature of the philosophical shift. Most historians agree that religious thought played an important role in the birth of modern science. To some extent it enabled or supported the movement that would become modern science. But religion's role in this shift is complicated, because religion encompasses a wide range of intellectual traditions.

Religious thought encompasses very different ideas, and this is exemplified no better than in the historical foundations of modern science. Two important names in the shift to modern science are Francis Bacon and René Descartes. Both were Christians, but their ideas about science could hardly have been more different. Bacon argued for limits to science, while Descartes argued for no limits to it. Bacon focused on the practical value of science, while Descartes promoted speculation in the sciences. And Bacon was an empiricist, while Descartes was a rationalist.

Given the significant differences between Bacon and Descartes, it is perhaps not surprising that science itself covers a wide spectrum of different activities. Parts of this spectrum strongly tend toward Bacon's empiricism—driven mostly by the data. Other parts tend toward Descartes' rationalism—driven more by ideology. This last point is often underappreciated. Science, the textbooks explain, is an activity rooted in empiricism. This textbook explanation is widespread, but it is simplistic and not always accurate.

Rationalism has been, and remains today, deeply embedded in parts of science. And while rationalism has its advantages, it also has its disadvantages. The point here is not that rationalism in science should necessarily be rejected but rather that its presence and its theological assumptions need to be clarified. Not only is rationalism deeply embedded in science, it brings with it theological assumptions that guide and constrain science.

Religious thought has influenced science in ways that are often not recognized. Whether the rationalistic influences in science are healthy is sometimes a difficult question. What is less controversial is that we need to understand the influence and implications of rationalism in science today. This chapter examines the origins of rationalism in modern science and its theological assumptions. Examples of its persistence will come in later chapters.

Francis Bacon

On a cold winter day in March 1626, Francis Bacon (1561–1626) wondered whether snow could be used to preserve animal flesh. He was driving his carriage near London and decided to investigate this practical idea. He stopped at a cottage along the way, purchased a chicken, and began stuffing it with snow. Unfortunately Bacon caught a chill and within days died from bronchitis. He was sixty-five years old. Bacon died doing what he had tirelessly advocated for years—learning about nature by observation and experimentation.

Bacon was born into an elite family of statesmen, but he flaunted wealth unwisely and was perpetually short of money. His father's premature death may have given him a rough start, but Bacon did not help matters by living ahead of his income. Twice he ran afoul of the law in money matters: once for his indebtedness and once for accepting bribes (though this was not an uncommon practice at the time).

It was this unlikely candidate who would become, for many, the father of modern science. In his teenage years at Trinity College, Bacon learned to despise Aristotelian philosophy. Aristotelianism was rationalistic. It tended to have preconceived notions of how nature works. Bacon studied several sciences at Trinity, and it seemed that Aristotelianism was the preconceived truth into which all data had to fit, no matter how awkward the fit.

Hence the idea of a clean slate in the sciences became important for Bacon. The clean slate would free science of preconceptions not based on empirical evidence. For Bacon it was obvious that general axioms ought to be the end, not the beginning, of the scientific process. In Bacon's inductive method, the scientist was to design experiments systematically and collect and tabulate the resulting data. All but one variable should be held constant so that the influences of each could be isolated. The observations were to be ordered in a set of tables that were meant to ensure progress toward certainty.[1] Bacon shunned any sort of speculation or hypothesis not grounded in observation.[2]

This included religious speculation. Bacon argued that religious considerations must not be unwisely mingled with natural science.[3] Bacon wanted to restrict science to a study of secondary causes—the workings of natural laws. He dismissed the concern that this would make science a breeding ground for heresy and atheism.[4] Bacon did see his scientific method as supplying its own knowledge via the senses, but this avenue was by no means sufficient to gain all knowledge. Questions of the human soul, for instance, were beyond its purview.[5] Nor could natural science reveal the image or will of God.

In Bacon's view, not only are there ultimate truths that science cannot delve into, but religious truth is also a remedy for bad science. Bacon warned that the real threat to science is not atheism or materialism but religious heresy. For religious ideas have far more power over the mind. Bacon was concerned that his induction method was vulnerable to such influences. Wise inquirers were needed to overcome these dangerous influences.[6] Great dangers awaited those scientists who practiced their profession without such virtues as humility and self-denial. Bacon certainly did not call for science to be independent of religion. For Bacon, science was religion's "most faithful handmaiden."[7]

Bacon saw two opposing problems that could stymie scientific research. The first was that religious speculation might interfere with science. Science ought not indulge in such metaphysical reasoning—it needed to be bounded within the limits of empiricism. At the other extreme, there were those who would go too far in limiting scientific research. At this extreme, natural knowledge was seen as dangerous because it plays into humanity's fallen nature and leads to pride and ambition. To avoid these pitfalls, some argued that empirical investigation of nature needed to be limited. Bacon argued against both extremes. He used the sun as a metaphor for how science should work, pursuing knowledge but only where appropriate:

> My first admonition (which was also my prayer) is that men confine the sense within the limits of duty in respect of things divine: for the sense is like the sun, which reveals the face of earth, but seals and shuts up the face of heaven. My next, that in flying from this evil they fall not into the opposite error, which they will surely do if they think that the inquisition of nature is in any part interdicted or forbidden.[8]

Religious reasoning must not be mingled with science, but this did not mean an investigation of nature was forbidden.

These concerns of Bacon are relevant today. Bacon was a prolific writer, and not all of his ideas would be easy to defend. But regarding the relationship between science and religion, he was often cogent. He did not imagine, as lesser thinkers would later assert, that science could be wholly apart from religion and free of its influence. He argued for a substantial relaxation of religion's role and for allowing science room to discover with a minimum of external constraint.

Bacon was not so naive as to think science could be completely severed from religion. Instead, he recognized that religion can have undue influence on science, and he argued for what he thought was an appropriate low level of influence. Unfortunately, this wisdom of Bacon was too often unappreciated. Having ignored his warnings and recommendations, today we have difficulties similar to what he hoped to avoid. Religious ideas indeed are powerful, and as we shall see, they have influenced science.

René Descartes

René Descartes (1596–1650) came a generation after Bacon, and, like Bacon, the French mathematician and philosopher rebelled against Aristotelianism. In Aristotelianism, phenomena were described in terms of qualities and forms. Fire, for example, had the quality of dryness and heat. But these are nothing more than descriptive labels. When such qualities are taken as *explanations* then problems arise, for we must then try to explain the explanations. As Descartes put it, "If you find it strange that . . . I do not use the qualities called 'heat,' 'cold,' 'moistness,' and 'dryness,' as do the philosophers, I shall say to you that these qualities appear to me to be themselves in need of explanation."[9] The qualities and forms failed to explain the physical action causing the effects. Instead, Descartes argued that science needed mechanical, or naturalistic, descriptions that could explain, rather than merely label, the effects.

Thus for Descartes naturalistic description was crucial. The size, shape, and motion of the matter involved was what counted. It was thought that matter occupied a volume of space, so for Descartes the fundamental quality of matter was extension, as opposed to a geometrical point, which has no volume. Extension gives rise to size, shape, and motion. It is these qualities, Descartes argued, that determine the gross qualities of matter—dryness, coldness, and so forth. For Descartes all matter was one and the same. It merely took on different forms as a consequence of its particular size, shape, and motion.

This was a profoundly different view of the world from that of the Aristotelians. In reaction to Aristotelianism, Descartes assumed matter was generic. It was like a sort of modeling clay made up of generic particles. The forms that seem apparent to us, such as water and fire, are merely transient manifestations of matter's configuration at the moment. For Descartes, matter had no innate forms. Water was water, and not fire, because the matter was in a different shape, not because the matter was fundamentally different.

Since particles are too small to be observed directly, it would be impossible to measure their actual sizes, shapes, and motions. The best investigators could do was hypothesize and check the plausibility of the guess. What science needed were naturalistic descriptions, even if they were not known to be true explanations. Thus Cartesian explanations were hypothetical; Descartes argued that having a plausible yet incorrect description was better than no description at all.

For the Cartesians, hypotheses might be inadequate or even known to be false. As Descartes wrote, when the true cause is unknown, "it suffices to imagine a cause which could produce the effect in question, even if it could have been produced by other causes and we do not know which is the true cause."[10] For Descartes, a theory could be fictional but still useful. He also applied a version of this logic to problems of cosmology. True, God created the universe, but a naturalistic description is nonetheless possible:

Even if in the beginning God had given the world only the form of a chaos, provided that he established the laws of nature and then lent his concurrence to enable nature to operate as it normally does, we may believe without impugning the miracle of creation that by this means alone all purely material things could in the course of time have come to be just as we now see them. And their nature is much easier to conceive if we see them develop gradually in this way than if we consider them only in their completed form.[11]

Hence the Cartesians set about constructing their many hypotheses. The hypotheses would be difficult or impossible to test, and they were based mostly on preconceptions about the world. As we shall see next, in later years Descartes' call for strictly naturalistic explanations would be canonized in science, but his justification would be replaced by another brand of rationalism.

Theological Naturalism

Both Bacon and Descartes reacted to Aristotelianism, but they did so in very different ways. Bacon urged that science replace rationalistic axioms—preconceived ideas about what must be true—with an empirical approach. Descartes argued for his own rationalistic axioms. The common thread was that both approaches focused on naturalistic explanations of nature. The world should be viewed as proceeding according to natural laws. But what are the limits of this approach? To what extent should this notion apply? Descartes' "useful fiction" idea—that naturalistic explanations should be used even when not true—is not very appealing. We shall see in this section that after Descartes, strong theological arguments were made for naturalism. These arguments claimed that science should be restricted to naturalistic explanations of nature not because they are useful fictions but because they are true.

By the beginning of the eighteenth century, naturalistic explanations in science were increasingly in vogue.[12] Historians well know that
the justification of the seventeenth century's naturalism involved nonscientific—theological—assumptions.[13] What is not always appreciated,
however, is how crucial these theological assumptions were in the move
to naturalism. As we shall see in this and later chapters, the theology
did not merely enable naturalism—it mandated naturalism, regardless
of how well the theories fit the data.

The theological mandates for naturalism fall into several categories.
Their common theme is that God ought not intervene in the creation and
care of the world. Nature should operate primarily, or even exclusively,
via natural laws, and it is not exclusively God's design. Naturalism in
the sciences did not arise from an empiricist urge; it arose from several
theological axioms and concerns. These concerns were not antireligious.
Though at times they were raised disingenuously by religious skeptics,
more often they were raised quite seriously by theists who were trying
to elucidate the relationship between God and creation.

These traditions, which I refer to as *theological naturalism*, are today as
powerful as they ever were. A common misconception is that theological
considerations were gradually dropped as modern science emerged in
the seventeenth century,[14] but actually the preference for naturalistic
explanations was, and remains, theologically motivated and justified.

Greater God

One important theological argument for naturalism is that it would
be clumsy for God to intervene against nature. God created the universe, so it hardly seems fitting that he would need to intervene in it. A
nonintervening God is a greater God.

This was the view of the Anglican cleric Thomas Burnet (1635–1715),
who authored the popular geologic work *Telluris Theoria Sacra* (*The Sacred Theory of the Earth*) in 1681. "We think him a better Artist," wrote
Burnet, "that makes a Clock that strikes regularly at every hour from

the Springs and Wheels which he puts in the work, than he that hath so made his Clock that he must put his finger to it every hour to make it strike."[15] In other words, special divine action should be minimized. It is better for God to create a self-sufficient machine than to make one needing divine intervention.

Isaac Newton was an exception. The solar system, with its planets and comets orbiting the Sun, was, for Newton, a "most beautiful system."[16] The laws of motion that Newton had discovered elegantly explained the motion of the planets and comets in their orbits. But Newton believed that these laws had their limits. Not only could they not construct the system in the first place but, due to rare interactions between the different celestial bodies, irregularities occur that are apt to increase until the system needs adjustment. According to Newton, the system on its own was not stable. The solar system would occasionally require, perhaps divine, intervention.[17]

It seemed to Newton that his natural laws could not be used to describe the creation or maintenance of the solar system. One virtue of this was that we would not be led astray by thinking God was unnecessary. The laws, by themselves, could not do the job. But others would object that this made God out to be a tinkerer and an unskilled creator. For in this view he would have created a machine that did not function properly.[18]

Burnet corresponded with Newton, as did the wide-ranging mathematician and philosopher Gottfried Leibniz (1646–1716). Leibniz was a devout Lutheran, and he accused Newton of disrespect for God in proposing the idea that God was not sufficiently skilled to create a self-sufficient clockwork universe.[19]

The great botanist John Ray (1627–1705) was an early English natural theologian who argued that creation revealed a divine design but not divine intervention. In his early-seventeenth-century work *The Wisdom of God Manifested in the Works of the Creation*, Ray argued that God would not "set his own hand as it were to every work, and immediately do all the meanest and trifling'st things himself drudgingly, without making use of any inferior or subordinate Minister."[20] For Ray, the details of nature were beneath God's concern. Better for nature itself to have a built-in creative capability.

Immanuel Kant (1724–1804) expounded upon this at length as an argument for naturalistic explanations for the origin of the cosmos. Kant was probably the most influential philosopher in the modern age, and in his early years he argued that it is most appropriate to the wisdom of God that the cosmic structures "develop themselves in an unforced succession out of the universal laws."[21] Fifty years later, at the end of the eighteenth century, Charles Darwin's grandfather Erasmus Darwin promoted this belief in more colorful prose:

> The world itself might have been generated, rather than created; that is, it might have been gradually produced from very small beginnings, increasing by the activity of its inherent principles, rather than by a sudden evolution by the whole by the Almighty fiat. What a magnificent idea of the infinite power of the great architect! The Cause of Causes! Parent of Parents! Ens Entium! For if we may compare infinities, it would seem to require a greater infinity of power to cause the causes of effects, than to cause the effects themselves.[22]

This religious sentiment was popular with scientists, theologians, and popularizers. In the nineteenth century, minister and professor John Playfair contended that James Hutton's uniformitarianism was far more conducive than instantaneous creation to reverent contemplation and a "properly worshipful attitude."[23] Likewise, Charles Lyell thought it more worthy of God to have designed interdependency to ensure balance and uniformity.[24] Robert Chambers wrote, "How can we suppose an immediate exertion of this creative power at one time to produce the zoophytes, another time to add a few marine mollusks, another to bring in one or two crustacea, again to crustaceous fishes, again perfect fishes, and so on to the end. This would surely be to take a very mean view of the Creative Power."[25] Divine providence was to engage in the noble activity of impressing laws upon matter, not constantly grovel in the muck of nature.

Descartes, Burnet, Leibniz, Ray, Kant, Hutton, Playfair, and Lyell are but a sampling of the many theists calling for naturalistic explanations in the years leading up to 1859, when Darwin published his theory of evolution. So it is hardly surprising that Darwin's theory would enjoy theological accolades. One of Darwin's early clerical supporters, the Anglican Charles Kingsley, provided one of the first such accolades after learning of Darwin's theory. "We knew of old that God was so wise that He could make all things but behold," wrote Kingsley, "He is so much wiser than even that, that He can make all things make themselves."[26]

Religious Rationalism and Deism

Does God give us truths that cannot be concluded from reason and logic, or is Christianity a belief that a thinking person can arrive at independent of scripture? This was a key question for seventeenth-century religious rationalism. The rationalists argued that religious belief is a logical conclusion. It was, they said, more a product of reason than an act of faith.

Rationalism sought to define a simplified version of Christianity. Those doctrines that could not be philosophically deduced were rejected—they were not part of what was referred to as *natural religion*. As one historian puts it, "What was 'reasonable' was also 'natural,' grounded somehow in the very nature of things. . . . Theological truth was arrived at not through religious experience but, rather, by logical deduction from certain first principles. The test of truth was that of rational consistency."[27]

It was from here only a short step, as Karl Barth pointed out, to all-out naturalism. In this religion of nature,[28] the world was to operate uniformly according to natural laws—theological truth depended on it. At the extreme of this movement were the deists. The deists claimed that anything requiring revelation and not grounded in natural religion was to be regarded as not divinely commanded and therefore not necessary for salvation and godly living.[29]

According to deism, religious truth should be deducible from nature rather than having to be revealed by God. Rather than being given at a particular time and place in history and then spreading throughout the world, God's revelation should be always available to all people in all places and at all times. Hence deism rejected the idea of a providential, active God. The workings of nature, rather than divine interventions, should provide the knowledge necessary for salvation. As the title of Matthew Tindal's 1730 book *Christianity as Old as the Creation* suggested, Christianity should not date back merely to the time of Christ. Since true religion is based more on nature than on revelation, Christianity should be as old as the creation.

In addition to the problem that revelation was not available to the entire human race, Tindal and the deists pointed out several other problems they perceived with the scriptures. Were they not full of inconsistencies and inaccuracies? And did the Bible not contain bad ethics and bad theology? Only natural religion provided a safe guide.[30]

One consequence of all this was that God's role was diminished. In the deist's view, it would be better to look to nature than to God's intervention for faith. Deism held to a sort of "clockmaker" creator, where God created the universe and its laws and then let it run like a clock without interference. But none of this stems from atheism or materialism. Today deism may seem one step away from religious skepticism, but the deists were by no means skeptics. They certainly rejected many of the traditional Christian doctrines, but they were motivated by theological concerns, not atheism. Their concern was theological, not atheological.

Another consequence of deistic thinking was that nature must be up to the task of salvation—it must be profound and pleasing rather than confusing. The young Kant, for example, argued that naturalism is required for our faith in the divine. What would we think of a Creator for "whom the universal natural laws obey only through some sort of compulsion and in and of themselves act counter to the plan of the Divinity's wisest designs"?[31] Instead, natural laws should do the creating so we can have certain "the proof of the Divinity":

The more perfect nature is in its developments, the better its universal laws lead to order and harmony, then the more certain the proof of the Divinity from which nature takes these relationships. Its productions are no longer the effects of contingency and results of accidents. Everything flows from it according to unchanging laws which thus must display nothing other than nature's skill, because they are exclusively features of the wisest of all designs from which disorder is prohibited. The chance collisions of the atoms of Lucretius did not develop the world. Implanted forces and laws which have their source in the Wisest Intelligence are an unchanging origin of that order inevitably flowing out from nature, not by chance, but by necessity.[32]

This argument for a naturalistic origin of the world was, according to Kant, based on "incontrovertible principles." And since nature reveals God's wisdom, it must be beautiful, perfect, and harmonious. This was Kant's message, and it was typical of the English natural theologians as well. They extolled the wonders and perfections of the natural world. Everything in creation was viewed as harmonious and perfectly fitted for the happiness of God's creatures.

Problem of Evil

It has been said that no one ever doubted the existence of God until philosophers tried to prove it. Sometimes those speaking for God try too hard and do more damage than good. A case in point are the English natural theologians who maintained that God's creation must be perfect and harmonious. It seems that the natural theologians were rather optimistic. What about the evil in the world? The natural theologians struggled to rationalize it or sometimes just ignored it. This movement is best known from the works of William Paley (1743–1805), but there were many others before and after him. The natural theologians argued that nature reveals a complex design, but they also argued for material perfection. As Paley put it, God "wills and wishes the happiness of His creatures."

Such emphasis on perfection and happiness only draws attention to what everyone intuitively knows: the world is far from a perfect and happy place. The natural theologians' optimistic view of the world supplied ample fodder for one of the strongest arguments of theological naturalism: the problem of evil. If God were all-powerful, all-knowing, and all-good, then the world would be perfect and free of evil. But since the world obviously is not free of evil, the premise must be false. God must not be the involved, take-charge sort of creator envisioned by classical theism. Whether this argument actually works is not important for our purposes. The point here is simply that this is another powerful theological argument for naturalistic explanations in science.[33]

In his *Dialogues concerning Natural Religion*, published posthumously in 1779, David Hume (1711–1776) wrote an engaging dialogue between three fictitious characters Cleanthes, Demea, and Philo, to make an argument for naturalism. Cleanthes, who represented the natural theologians, argues that the world was a happy place and that this is evidence for God. Hume has an easy time ridiculing this view. Philo, who represents Hume, and Demea agree that "a perpetual war is kindled amongst all living creatures" and that nature is so arranged so as "to embitter the life of every living being."[34] What is needed, Hume argued, is a transcendent God who is not involved in nature. This would explain how the world can be so evil.

Cleanthes's design argument is powerful. Philo admits the argument is a great challenge for him, but it is neutralized by the evil in the world. "I needed all my skeptical and metaphysical subtlety to elude your grasp," admits Philo, but "here I triumph."

This need to distance God and invoke natural causes as the source of the world's evils was felt long before Hume. For Thomas Burnet, Earth's geology revealed "a World lying in its rubbish."[35] Likewise, John Ray was concerned about nature's "errors and bungles."[36] Ray saw the powerful signs of God's design in nature. But for Ray, while the wonders of nature reveal a design from the mind of God, the problems of nature reveal a process of creation independent of God. Influenced by Ralph

Cudworth (1617–1688) of the Cambridge Platonists, Ray called for a "Plastic Nature" that evolves on its own, sometimes causing imperfect results. The wide influence of the problem of evil can be seen among natural theologians such as Ray and skeptics like Hume. The result was a powerful argument for naturalism in the historical sciences.

Similarly, as we shall see in chapter 8, Darwin made powerful arguments for his theory of evolution using nature's apparent dysteleology and evil. These strong arguments for evolution have persisted ever since his time. Today Ken Miller asks the rhetorical question, would God "really want to take credit for the mosquito"?[37] To him the answer is obvious. Similarly, the eminent evolutionary biologist Francisco Ayala calls it blasphemy to believe in the creation of the species. Ayala, a former Dominican priest, points to design flaws such as wisdom teeth that need to be removed as proof God did not create the species.[38] He writes: "There are too many deficiencies, too much cruelty in the world of life. To assume that they have been explicitly created by God amounts to blasphemy. I believe God to be omniscient and benevolent. The 'design' of organisms is not compatible with such beliefs."[39]

Against Miracles

Another development that paralleled deism was a growing sentiment against supernatural miracles. In the early eighteenth century this debate raged in England, and once again theological concerns were at the center of the move toward naturalism. Thomas Wollaston and Peter Annet, for instance, put forth a series of arguments against miracles, and their tracts numbered in the tens of thousands.[40] Wollaston ridiculed the idea of Jesus casting devils out of a madman and into a herd of pigs (Luke 8:26–39): "I could even now laugh at the thoughts of the Hoggs running and tumbling down-hill as if the Devil drove them."[41] To this Annet added a deistic concern regarding the resurrection of Jesus. If Jesus's resurrection was crucial for our salvation, then it should be better documented:

Is it probable that an extraordinary action done for an extraordinary end, and highly necessary to be known to mankind, should be so secretly done, that no man saw it! That so great an action should be done in so improper a way! That Jesus should require the men to believe his Disciples, rather than their own sense, in an affair where reason can be of no assistance![42]

Like the deists, Wollaston and Annet found divine intervention, this time in the form of miracles, to be theologically awkward. God has infinite knowledge, including foreknowledge, and power and wisdom. Hence God must be capable of so arranging and designing the natural order from eternity so as to accomplish his aims without violating the natural order.[43] And if God *can* get by without miracles, then God *would* get by without miracles. For rationalists, God would use miracles only if he needed to use them. As one historian recently explained:

Why is Wollaston prepared to go to such lengths to rule out the possibility of a miraculous violation of the laws of nature? The answer is suggested by some of the adjectives by which he describes the order of nature, e.g., "*noble* system"; Wollaston believes, like all true rationalists, that there is nobility and intrinsic perfection in regularity and order. Consequently, a world not perfectly ordered and regular in its operation would be an imperfect world and therefore its creator would be imperfect.[44]

Furthermore, as Annet argued, God's immutability mandates naturalism. God was the cause, and the laws of nature were the effect. A change in the effect—the natural order—means a change in the cause. But God does not change. And if such a change were required, it would reveal a blundering creator, or worse:

If God ever determined for moral ends and reasons to interpose, if needful, by a different method, than that of his standard laws; it must be either because he could not foresee the consequences, which is like blundering in the dark; or he foresaw it would be needful; and then it would be like a blunder in the design and contrivance; or he foreknew and determined his own works should not answer His own ends, without His mending work, which is worst of all.[45]

Annet also argued against miracles on the basis of the emerging tradition of uniformitarianism. This reasoning sounds more scientific, as it relies on the steady action of natural laws. Had not Newton showed that nature operates according to such laws? The fact that Newton himself did not interpret his findings as mandating naturalism did not seem to matter. For Annet, miracles are utterly impossible because they contradict the natural laws that are known from common experience. Jesus is said to have risen from the dead, but "we know by experience that all men must die, and rise no more, therefore we conclude, for a dead man to rise to life again, is contrary to the uniform and settled course of nature."[46] Both sense and reason inform us that it is impossible for a dead body to live again: "To believe it possible contradicts this maxim, *That nature is steady and uniform in her operations*."[47]

The not-too-subtle problem here is that this reasoning ultimately is circular. Hume later refined and expanded this argument from uniformitarianism. Though Hume's arguments were largely failures, they would not be recognized as such.[48] As one philosopher has commented, "I find it astonishing how well posterity has treated 'Of Miracles,' given how completely the confection collapses under a little probing."[49] The logic may have been lacking, but the move toward naturalism and uniformitarianism did not arise from logical deduction. Its popularity is less surprising when we see the underlying theological motivations. Indeed, there is much more to this story. Various theological maneuverings often led to minimization or sometimes outright dismissal of miracles.[50] The point here is simply that theological concerns often motivated a move toward naturalistic explanations.

In the years following Hume, miracles were increasingly rejected on such grounds. Henry Peter Brougham (1778–1868), Lord Chancellor of England and advocate of natural theology, argued that miracles proved nothing but the exercise of miraculous power and they left the creator's trustworthiness in question.[51] Scottish social reformer George Combe (1788–1858) also suspected that the picture of a continually interfering God was flawed. He argued that God governs through unchangeable laws and not supernatural interventions.[52]

The Ground Rules

The acceptance and influence of Hume's arguments against miracles signaled the next logical step in the progression toward naturalism. As we have seen, theological naturalism was pressed on several fronts. But soon it became something like a self-fulfilling prophecy as evidence was interpreted *according to* naturalism and then seen as *supporting* naturalism. Science, it was said, has revealed a mechanistic world. In fact, the evidence did not reveal this; rather, the evidence was interpreted this way.

Naturalism began to be viewed as a scientifically established principle, and by the second half of the nineteenth century it was seen as a sort of scientific fact. At Oxford the Reverend Professor Baden Powell concluded that science had confirmed "the grand truth of the universal order and constancy of natural causes as a primary law of belief."[53] On the assumptions of naturalism and the continuity of natural laws, Powell wrote, "the whole superstructure of rational geology entirely reposes: to deny them in any instance would be to endanger all science."[54] Similarly, in 1888, Berkeley professor Joseph Le Conte linked naturalism with the very validity of reason:

> The origins of new phenomena are often obscure, even inexplicable, but we never think to doubt that they have a natural cause; for so to doubt is to doubt the validity of reason, and the rational constitution of Nature. So also, the origins of new organic forms may be obscure or even inexplicable, but we ought not on that account to doubt that they had a natural cause, and came by a natural process; for so to doubt

is also to doubt the validity of reason, and the rational constitution of organic Nature.[55]

George Romanes wrote in 1878 that naturalism can explain "any of the phenomena of the universe," and botanist Karl von Nägeli explained that "everything can be explained in a natural way."[56] In the twentieth century the French Jesuit paleontologist and philosopher Pierre Teilhard de Chardin (1881–1955) described Darwin's theory of evolution as no mere theory or hypothesis, but "a general postulate to which all theories, all hypotheses, all systems must henceforward bow and which they must satisfy in order to be thinkable and true."[57]

Of course these views were not universally accepted and were not without at least some controversy when they were first proposed. At each step, this movement I am calling theological naturalism had its detractors. From Burnet to Powell, the theological naturalists were routinely met with the charge of atheism or its equivalent.[58] But while one may disagree with theological naturalism, one should not simply label it as atheism or materialism. The arguments and premises were theological, as the concern was how to understand the relationship between God and creation.

The point here is not that theological naturalism is right or wrong. To argue either way would require a theological treatise. The point here is simply that naturalism was driven by theological concerns, and we will see many more examples of this in later chapters. Further, the point is not that theological naturalism equates with materialism or *metaphysical naturalism*. Quite the opposite: theological naturalism is based on theism, not atheism. Theological naturalism is not opposed to all things religious—it *is* religious. Theological naturalism mandates a nonintervening god; it does not mandate no god. It means that divine action must not be empirically detectable. Hence theological naturalism mandates *methodological naturalism*—the idea that science ought to pursue naturalistic explanations. It is not that there is no god but that creation must always operate according to uniform natural laws.

To be sure, there also were religious skeptics who argued for naturalism, but even they relied on either the success of theological naturalism or the premises of theological naturalism. Hume, for example, drew extensively from religious sentiment in arguing for naturalism. He rejected the claim that complexity mandates a designer, for instance, because this reasoning reduces God to our level by making him out to be a sort of craftsman rather than the infinitely superior being that he is:

> But as all perfection is entirely relative, we ought never to imagine that we comprehend the attributes of this divine being, or to suppose that his perfections have any analogy or likeness to the perfections of a human creature. Wisdom, thought, design, knowledge; these we justly ascribe to him; because these words are honorable among men, and we have no other language or other conceptions by which we can express our adoration of him. But let us beware, lest we think that our ideas anywise correspond to his perfections, or that his attributes have any resemblance to these qualities among men. He is infinitely superior to our limited view and comprehension; and is more the object of worship in the temple, than of disputation in the schools.[59]

Regardless of Hume's true feelings, here and elsewhere he often relied on the premises of theological naturalism. As nineteenth-century historian W. E. H. Lecky pointed out, eighteenth-century deism was largely devoid of arguments derived from the discoveries of physical science.[60]

Naturalism is not a finding of science. Newton's finding that the planets orbit the sun according to a uniform natural law does not mean the cosmos must have been exclusively formed by natural laws. And so there are two errors to avoid in characterizing the historical science's move to naturalism. The move to naturalism is neither atheism in disguise nor a scientific discovery. Instead, the move to naturalism was mandated largely by thinkers within the church. Religious skeptics gladly accepted the move, but their position has always been a parasitic one.

The mechanistic philosophy predated the mechanistic theories. Indeed, though our focus here is on modern science, mechanistic philosophies date back to antiquity. Epicurus, for instance, sought mechanistic explanations to satisfy his concerns about the problem of evil, morality, and religious superstition. And the ancient mechanical philosophies had their modern-era sympathizers, such as Pierre Gassendi (1592–1655).[61] All of this suggests a contingency in today's assumption of naturalism. The assumption of naturalism is justified by nonscientific, metaphysical concerns.

There is a misconception that modern science is free of religious concerns. Did not Bacon and Descartes oust Aristotelianism in favor of a naturalistic philosophy? Yes, but this switch introduced a new set of religious assumptions. The seventeenth century did not free science of religious influence, it merely changed the influence. Aristotelianism was out, theological naturalism was in. The revolution did not free science of metaphysics, it merely changed the metaphysic.

3

Science's Blind Spot

Imagine trying to predict the stock market. One person might think about the problem and devise rules for how the market ought to behave. If unemployment rises, then the stock market should decline. If earnings rise, then stock prices should gain. Another person might set about collecting all the relevant economic data from past decades and then search for correlations. Stocks may rise or they may fall when unemployment rises—who knows?

In this simple example the first person uses a *rational* approach whereas the second person uses an *empirical* approach. In science both approaches may be used depending on the problem at hand, availability of data, type of result needed, and thinking style of the scientist. At the extremes, purely rational and purely empirical approaches are not practical. One cannot expect to make very much progress by simply thinking about a problem. And one cannot measure and interpret data without assuming something about the data. Science, like our every-day decision making, is a combination of rationalism and empiricism. There are some assumptions made (rationalism), and observations are used (empiricism). But the assumptions could be false. They cannot be proved by science. Rather, the assumptions are above the science—they are metaphysical.

The ideal in science is to reduce the rationalism and its assumptions to a bare minimum. Science is to be driven by the evidence in the natural world, not by how we think the world should work. As Darwin's friend Thomas H. Huxley wrote, "The scientist must sit down before fact as a little child, be prepared to give up every preconceived notion, follow humbly wherever and to whatever abysses nature leads, or you shall learn nothing." But this is an ideal from which science sometimes strays. As we shall see in later chapters, Darwin's theory of evolution, which Huxley so strenuously advocated, was based on the assumptions of theological naturalism. Evolution was hardly the empirical ideal that Huxley espoused.

This chapter examines where, in the wide spectrum of scientific thought, rationalism tends to predominate. What we will find is that theological naturalism brings with it an inevitable blind spot which today's science lacks the resources to reckon with.

Naturalism in the Historical Sciences

In centuries past the theory of spontaneous generation was used to explain maggots in rotting meat and rats in open garbage dumps. The maggots and rats seemed inevitable. Did not the garbage give rise to rats and meat to maggots? Spontaneous generation was eventually disproved by Louis Pasteur in the nineteenth century, and with its passing, biology embraced the law of biogenesis, which stated that all life comes only from preexisting life: *omne vivum ex vivo*.

But if this is true, then how did life begin? Naturalists agree that life had a beginning. And if life had a beginning, then it has *not* always come from preexisting life. The law of biogenesis, it seems, is not really a law. Or shall we say, the law of biogenesis is a law of limited application.

There are other examples like this. For instance, science has found that disorder always increases in the universe and stars form from other stars. These findings also seem to have limited application. For disorder always to increase, there must have been order at the start. Order must first have increased for it to decrease. Likewise, the very first stars must have formed not from other stars.

In the experimental sciences, naturalism has been tremendously successful. Bacon and Descartes may not have had all the details correct, but their vision led to a prolific enterprise. Modern science has revolutionized everyday life. Its inventions are now so pervasive that they are often taken for granted. It is hard to imagine, for instance, what life would be like without electric lights.

We have detailed and often convincing explanations for how things work. We can explain and predict phenomena with reductionist explanations involving masses, energy, forces, and the like. What about the historical sciences? Is there a bridge between the experimental and historical sciences? Can we not extrapolate our fantastic success in explaining phenomena in the laboratory into natural history?

Newton explained the ellipses that the planets trace out as a simple consequence of the sun's gravitational influence. Thus, it is no surprise that the planets travel in ellipses about the sun, as Johannes Kepler had earlier observed. A century after Newton, it seemed that even perturbations to this system would be self-correcting. The story was complex, but it was also naturalistic. Could we not then, as the great French mathematician and physicist Pierre Laplace (1749–1827) argued, regard the present state of the universe as the effect of its antecedent state and as the cause of the state that is to follow?[1]

Laplace believed the future is determined by the past. It could be predicted given sufficient computing power and complete knowledge of all the masses at some previous time. When Napoleon asked Laplace why he wrote so much about the universe but nothing about the creator, Laplace is said to have replied, "I had no need of that hypothesis."[2]

Naturalism was steadily becoming a fact, and it encompassed both experimental and historical sciences. The two were bridged as natural history was viewed as one long Laplacean experiment. This was a persuasive and powerful idea for the sanctioning of naturalism in the historical sciences. The nineteenth-century philosopher John Stuart Mill argued that hypothesizing in the historical sciences is "an example of legitimate reasoning from a present effect to a possible past cause, according to the known laws of that cause."[3] Darwin concluded his book on evolution with an appeal to this notion of planets tracing out their paths according to gravity, as a context in which to view his theory of biological wonders arising from simple laws. "There is a grandeur in this view of life, with its several powers, having been originally breathed by the Creator into a few forms or into one; and that, whilst this planet has gone cycling on according to the fixed law of gravity, from so simple a beginning endless forms most beautiful and most wonderful have been, and are being evolved."[4]

In other words, Darwin argued for an uninterrupted continuum of natural history. Indeed, for theological naturalists there must be an uninterrupted continuum. There must be no principled distinction between the experimental and historical sciences. Natural laws that explain how the planets move must also be sufficient to explain how they originated. Order somehow arose in the universe, and the first stars and life somehow developed. For naturalists this must be true. Our complex world, they say, must unfold as a result of the interplay of natural laws.

The Historical and Experimental Sciences

Consider the case of two researchers who are both life scientists but do very different work. One tries to figure out how nerve cells work, the other tries to figure out how amphibians evolved from fish. The first scientist performs laboratory experiments to learn more about nerve cells. The second scientist reconstructs hypothetical events in the distant history of life. These two types of work make for very different types of science.

One difference lies in the *assumption of uniformity*. Our experimental scientist requires a certain level of uniformitarianism. The laboratory scientist assumes that past experiments are valid today and that the same natural laws apply everywhere. But as the law of biogenesis illustrates, much more is implied when our historical scientist makes the assumption of uniformity. In addition to the assumptions the laboratory scientist makes, this scientist must extrapolate back in time to earlier epochs when no observers were present.

Imagine if extraterrestrials visited this planet and discovered the four faces carved out of Mt. Rushmore. How wrong they would be to assume the faces were carved by nothing but the uniform action of natural processes. One could construct a theory for how natural processes such as erosion formed the four faces. The theory would likely not work very well, because the faces were not carved by such processes. Obviously, the fact that the same natural laws apply across time and space does not mean that *all* phenomena can and must be explainable by these laws. The assumption of uniformity is by no means guaranteed to be true.

A theory of how the Mt. Rushmore faces were formed by naturalistic processes would have plenty of anomalies—features in the data that the theory could not explain very well. In the experimental sciences, such *data anomalies* can often serve as motivation for further research. The anomaly that occurs only under certain conditions but otherwise is unexplained by the theory may be the clue to a new and better theory. In the historical sciences, as we shall see in chapters 4–6, anomalies are easily tolerated and even ignored as some kind of statistical noise.

Anomalies make *theory evaluation* difficult for our historical scientist. How is one to judge a historical theory that fails to explain certain parts of the data? Those anomalies are typically explained with reference to one-time, contingent events or simply ignored. As we shall see in a moment, theories in the experimental sciences do not typically use contingent events as explanatory mechanisms.

Imagine that a scientist hypothesizes the earth is flat and tests the theory by predicting how far a cannonball will fly. The predictions are not quite right. Part of the prediction error comes from the experimental process itself. Wind, atmospheric density, and other factors cannot be controlled or exactly measured. Nor can the flight of the cannonball be exactly measured. But all these error sources can be quantified and used to caveat the experimental results. The measurements are understood not to be exact. The range of the cannonball is measured to be a certain distance, plus or minus an error factor. And when the predictions are consistently outside the range of possible values, then scientists do not blame the conditions. The theory may be useful, even though it consistently produces a small, mysterious error. But the scientist knows there is an error. The scientist will blame the theory rather than conjure up complicated, one-time stories to explain the particular prediction error that resulted in each firing of the cannon.

In the historical sciences it is easier to employ one-time events that could have caused what we observe in the data. For instance, fossils that appear abruptly in the geological strata can be said to be the result of an extremely fast evolutionary process that left no earlier fossils. Unlike in the cannon experiments, we have no way of knowing that such one-time events did, or did not, occur in the distant past when no observers were present. Such events may be very unlikely, but that does not mean they did not occur. It is difficult to evaluate the likelihood of these events, and hence it is difficult to evaluate the likelihood that the theory is true, or approximately true. On the other hand, in the flat earth theory example above, the evidence was strong that the theory was false (though the theory could nonetheless be useful).

The question of *repeatability* reveals yet another typical difference in the work of our experimental and historical scientists. Textbooks and scientists alike consistently maintain that science must be limited to repeatable observations.[5] There are many reasons for this requirement.

For instance, it ensures that science is not beholden to private knowledge. If an observation cannot be independently verified, then it is not used. It also means that experimental errors can be uncovered. More subtle is investigator interference. It can be tempting for scientists to guide the experiment, perhaps ever so slightly, to reach the desired results. There is also the possibility of outright forgery. All these missteps can be avoided by requiring that observations be repeatable.

But in spite of all this and in spite of what the textbooks claim, science does accept observations that are not repeatable. Sometimes repeatability is simply not possible. Paleontology, for instance, involves observations of fossils. If a particular fossil is unique, then the observations are not repeatable. The infamous Piltdown hoax occurred when a fossil forgery from an archaeological site in England was accepted as an intermediate fossil species. The Piltdown hoax illustrates the difficulty that the historical sciences sometimes face in the use of one-time "observations" that cannot be repeated.[6]

In addition to the problem of repeating observations, there is the fact that in the experimental sciences the phenomenon under study often can be experimented upon any number of times under a variety of conditions. And when such repeated experimentation is not possible, such as in much of astronomy, nature often provides the experiments for us. From stars to galaxies and quasars, celestial objects are usually presented to us in great variety. It is almost like being able to repeat the experiment.

In the historical sciences, on the other hand, the phenomenon under study often cannot be repeated experimentally. How are we to repeat the formation of the universe, for instance? How are we to repeat the evolution of a now-extinct fossil species leading to another? Evolutionary events are "unique, unrepeatable, and irreversible," in the words of Theodosius Dobzhansky. Or as Ernst Mayr writes, "Darwin introduced historicity into science. Evolutionary biology, in contrast with physics and chemistry, is a historical science—the evolutionist attempts to explain events and processes that have already taken place. Laws and experiments are inappropriate techniques" for explaining evolutionary events and processes.[7]

This leads to another distinction between our two scientists, regarding how one-time *contingencies* are treated. Unlike the experimental sciences, the historical sciences make liberal use of one-time contingent causes to explain the data. This is another reason that repeatability is not important in the historical sciences. Rather than events being driven by the necessities of lawlike processes, they are viewed as the chance effects of contingencies. Natural history is viewed as caused by a great many random events. In the experimental sciences, on the other hand, theory is expected to be sufficient to explain what we observe. The view of contingencies could hardly be more different between the experimental and historical sciences.

In fact, the free use of contingency is the basis for important evidences cited for naturalistic theories. As we shall see in later chapters, patterns found in nature are explained as having been caused by contingent causes. These are not mere explanations—they are cited as powerful evidence for naturalistic theories. Contingencies are crucial in the historical sciences. But in the experimental sciences they have no place.

On the empiricism-versus-rationalism scale, another important distinction is that our experimental scientist tends more toward empiricism while our historical scientist tends more toward rationalism. Dealing with limited observability of events in the distant past, the historical scientist will need to make more assumptions about the problem. Today, theological naturalism is the basis for such assumptions.

Science's Blind Spot

Science spans a great diversity of research activities. These cannot all be neatly classified as being "experimental" or "historical." But there is a significant difference in the assumptions and methods across this spectrum of activities. The fact that we have mastered chemistry and physics in the laboratory should not convince us that we necessarily can describe all of natural history. We know how planets orbit and chemicals react, but this knowledge does not translate to certain understanding of how the planets and molecules arose in the first place. The best we can hope for is to demonstrate plausible explanations. Victor Stenger echoes Descartes when he writes that what science needs are "plausible scenarios for a fully material universe, even if those scenarios cannot be currently tested."[8]

Stenger's call for plausible naturalistic explanations is quite reasonable. It is obvious that we cannot perfectly retrace history's devious paths, so who would disagree that a feasible and plausible naturalistic explanation, even if it could never be proved to be true, ought to be accepted? Only nonscientific opposition would stand in the way of such a solution.

This leaves only one issue to be resolved: how do we judge whether a theory is plausible? Imagine, for a moment, something that is not the result strictly of natural processes. Is it possible that such a thing exists? Could there be something—love, consciousness, soul, life, or whatever—that is the result of something more than matter in motion?

The answer to this hypothetical question would seem obviously to be yes. Of course it is *possible* that such things exist. Yet theological naturalism has so taken hold that even this admission is often difficult to obtain. I am always surprised, when I ask this question, that many scientists believe science has somehow proved to us that such phenomena, in fact, do not exist.

But science has shown us no such thing. There is no experiment or proof that demonstrates that naturalism is the source of everything we observe. It is possible that nonnaturalistic phenomena exist, and it is not a good sign that this needs explaining.

Now given the fact that such phenomena might exist, it follows that naturalism might struggle in explaining them. There is an old school-yard game in which a person is shown several rolls of a pair of dice. With each roll he is told what number he should deduce, according to a secret code. He observes several rolls and tries to figure out the code.

But his guesses always come up short, because the code does not use the die values. With each roll of the die the roller folds his arms, each time hiding some fingers and making others visible. Unbeknownst to the observer, the number produced by each event is simply the number of visible fingers. The result is contingent on the choice of the roller—there is no rationale involving the dice.

If there are phenomena that do not reduce to naturalistic explanations, then theological naturalism would be tricked as well. If such phenomena exist, then in those cases naturalistic explanations of them could never be true explanations. At best they would be constructs—made-up stories to describe and predict aspects of the phenomena in question.

Imagine a scientist who begins to study a nonnatural phenomenon. She is unaware that the phenomenon is not natural, and since today's science seeks only naturalistic explanations, she confines her research accordingly. Perhaps her naturalistic explanations, though not true in this case, can nonetheless somewhat accurately describe the phenomenon and make some useful predictions. In this case naturalism works just fine.

But what if not? What if, as in the schoolyard game, the naturalistic explanations are forever stymied—stymied because they use natural laws and processes to describe a phenomenon that does not follow such laws and processes? By searching and searching, the scientist may find a partial fit. So she may have some success, but there are always unexplained observables—data anomalies for which the naturalistic explanation cannot account. In this case naturalistic explanations will always be problematic. More data will be collected, further analysis will be done, and theories will be modified or replaced altogether. All good scientific research and—in our hypothetical example of a nonnatural phenomenon—wrong.

The problem with science is not that the naturalistic approach might occasionally be inadequate. The problem is that science would never know any better. This is science's blind spot. When problems are encountered, theological naturalism assumes that the correct naturalistic solution has not yet been found. Nonnatural phenomena will be interpreted as natural, regardless of how implausible the story becomes. Science has no mechanism to detect the possibility of nonnatural phenomena. It does not consider the likelihood that a phenomenon might not be purely naturalistic.

Consider the following example. What if it were found that a code existed in all living species and that, within each organism, complicated machinery was used to read vast amounts of stored information via the code? Say the machinery was so complicated that it *automatically* (1) read the information, (2) used the code to interpret the information, and (3) acted on the instructions. And what if, after decades of research, no naturalistic explanation could be found for how the code and machinery arose?[9]

Even in this example, scientists would have to continue to search for only naturalistic explanations. There are many problems with naturalistic explanations for the existence of the code and associated machinery. The problem seems to defy naturalistic explanation. But there *must be* a plausible explanation for how the code arose which has not yet been discovered. This is, of course, no hypothetical example. The DNA code, discovered and elucidated several decades ago, has defied plausible naturalistic explanation, but it fuels an ongoing and growing research community of historical scientists in the origin-of-life field.

Theological naturalism has no way to distinguish a paradigm problem from a research problem. It cannot consider the *possibility* that there is no naturalistic explanation for the DNA code. If a theory of natural history has problems—and many of them have their share—the problems are always viewed as research problems and never as paradigm problems.

Theological naturalists restrict themselves to naturalistic explanations because they must. Like Sisyphus forever pushing the stone up the hill, they must pursue naturalistic explanations no matter how unlikely, for theological naturalism has no criteria, no set of rules by which to distinguish a research problem from a paradigm problem. This helps to explain the hesitancy of some scientists to admit that nonnatural phenomena might exist. They follow Descartes' prescription and approach everything using naturalistic explanations, sometimes forgetting the limits under which they work. It also helps to explain the tolerance for improbable theories. The strict adherence to naturalism sometimes leads to unlikely explanations.

What if Francis Bacon was right? What if there is a line that, when crossed, renders a naturalistic explanation no better than the schoolboy guessing at the die? Then on the other side of that line theological naturalism would be a fool's errand—and it would never know it.

A Four-Way Intersection

Historian Thomas Kuhn has pointed out that science tends to work in paradigms.[10] Researchers ask questions within the paradigm rather than on the veracity of the paradigm. The paradigm is taken for granted. In this sense, each paradigm has a sort of blind spot. Rather than considering how each piece of evidence bears on the paradigm itself, researchers seek to incorporate the evidence within the paradigm as best as possible.

The grand, overriding paradigm in the historical sciences today is theological naturalism. Across the various fields of study, the common requirement is that explanations be naturalistic. And in this grand paradigm there is a grand blind spot. Problems are never interpreted as problems with the paradigm. No matter how implausible, when explanations do not fit the data very well, they are said to be research problems. They must be, for there is no option for considering that a problem might be better handled by another paradigm.

It is no revelation that science has its paradigms and that there might be a narrowing, rather than widening, of scientific thought within paradigms. What is less well recognized is that today's science has a blind spot. For cannot scientists hold to naturalism tentatively? No, theological naturalism assumes that what we observe in the world *must* have arisen from natural causes. Theological naturalists do not evaluate any other possibility, for it is blind to any such possibility. It presupposes that naturalism is true, regardless of the scientific evidence.

In most cases this idea of a blind spot is foreign to the scientist. In fact most are under the impression that science has searched and not found any evidence for nonnaturalistic phenomena. As naturalists Maitland Edey and Donald Johanson wrote, "If our scientific inquiry should lead eventually to God . . . that will be the time to stop science."[11] The typical belief among scientists is not that there is a blind spot but rather that science and its naturalism can and does positively search for the nonnatural.

The blind spot inherent in naturalism is not commonly discussed in the sciences. The scientist, whose job is to construct explanations for the natural world, is not typically concerned that the project may have limits. Nor is he typically aware of the historical contingency of naturalism. Naturalism is not a discovery of science—it is a presupposition of science as currently practiced. It is a metaphysical assumption that arose over time in the history of ideas, motivated by several religious arguments. If those arguments are true, then all is well with the historical sciences, but we have no assurance of this.

The scientist, however, views naturalism not as a historical contingency but as a discovery of science. So it is understandable that he resists any notion of a blind spot. The historian, on the other hand, understands the historical contingency of naturalism. She knows that naturalism arose within the history of ideas and that, like any idea, it might have its limits.

But the historian also knows that in the experimental sciences there has been an inexorable march of progress. Over the centuries, discoveries and inventions have continued to mount. Surely this is no coincidence. There must be some truth to naturalism. What the historian does not appreciate is the distinction between the experimental and historical sciences. She is not suspicious that the impressive success of naturalism in the former assures the latter of very little.

The theologian sees a terrible confusion occurring. The scientist and historian may be correct that science will not be stopped, and nothing in the material world is beyond its reach, but God is something else altogether. Therefore, one should not think scientific explanations of the world can crowd out God.

The theologian's concern is that some believers may seek to intertwine the divine with the natural world. Where naturalistic explanations are weak, this is where supernatural explanations are needed, these believers may think. But if this strengthens our faith, then it will equally damage our faith when naturalism later fills in the gaps of our knowledge. When God is used to explain gaps in science, we have a God of the gaps. And as the gaps are closed we are left with no God at all.

According to the theologian, we must never use God as the explanation where naturalistic explanations have not yet succeeded. For as the historian warns, those explanations will eventually succeed, and God will be crowded out.

This is yet another powerful argument for naturalism in science, in addition to those we saw in chapter 2. As Thomas Burnet warned in the seventeenth century, "'Tis a dangerous thing to engage the authority of Scripture in disputes about the Natural World, in opposition to Reason, lest Time, which brings all things to light, should discover that to be false which we made Scripture to assert."[12]

The philosopher, whose job is to explain how we think and know, is less impressed with the claims of science. He knows that a scientist's statement that something is true does not make it true. Not only are scientific theories suspect of being unprovable, but they might even be nothing more than useful fiction. Instead of providing descriptions of the underlying reality, perhaps scientific theories are merely constructs, employing entities that have no existence in reality.

But the philosopher is concerned that naturalism in the historical sciences is attacked by religious activists. It seems these activists are less concerned with the health of science than with the *results* of science. The results contradict their religious beliefs, so they call for a change in science. They want to curb naturalism, not to improve science but so that its discoveries can be controlled. This is an abuse of science. Where the theologian worries that questioning naturalism harms our faith, the philosopher worries that it harms our knowledge. It seems that the scientist, historian, theologian, and philosopher all have concerns that naturalism can help resolve. The urge for purely naturalistic explanations in science is understandable.

The Confusion over Naturalism

The assumption of naturalism in the sciences is often misunderstood. The term *naturalist* is today often taken to refer to atheists and materialists. But this ignores the great many theists, of one sort or another, who advocate naturalistic explanations. They advocate naturalistic explanations because they believe in a nonintervening god. The sentiment that motivates naturalism is itself deeply religious. This leads to *methodological* naturalism but not to *metaphysical* naturalism (i.e., materialism).

These powerful arguments are not easily countered, and for critics of naturalism there is a certain attraction to the naturalism-equals-atheism model. If naturalism can be reduced to religious cynicism, then it is stripped of those powerful arguments. For these critics, naturalism becomes the result of dysfunctional faith rather than compelling metaphysical contentions. But the criticism is misplaced. Instead of recognizing naturalism as an attempt to resolve difficult theological concerns, these critics cast it as nothing more than the bad fruit of atheism. Better to describe the world as intricate and complex and ascribe naturalism to religious infidelity.

To be sure, atheists such as Steven Weinberg and Richard Dawkins have enjoyed the rise of naturalism. And atheists have employed the metaphysical justifications as well as anyone, whether or not these atheists actually believe those justifications. But the atheists are a side show; the mandate for naturalism in science arose from theism, not atheism.

The naturalism-equals-atheism model fits neither the history of naturalism nor the state of naturalism today. Nonetheless, from Charles

Hodge in the nineteenth century to Alvin Plantinga today, it persists.[13] And when it is arises, the naturalist has a ready answer: "Sorry, but I'm not an atheist."

Plantinga urges that theists ought to use all their knowledge in their scientific pursuits. What we know about God should be incorporated in our theorizing.[14] But this is precisely what naturalists *have* been doing. It is not the case that the historical sciences lack a fully orbed research program that includes all our knowledge—metaphysical and physical. There is an abundance of religious and metaphysical theorizing.

What we need, to begin with, is a clear understanding of what naturalism is. Naturalism's adherents think it is a scientific discovery, and its detractors think it is atheism in disguise. In fact, it is a rationalist movement built on a foundation of religious thought and traditions that mandate a world that operates according to natural laws and processes. In this theological naturalism, religious justifications are freely used, but all explanations must be naturalistic. There are problems with many naturalistic explanations, but this is not why naturalism is ailing. It is ailing because it cannot contemplate the possibility that it may be wrong. It cannot evaluate these problems from a larger perspective. Naturalistic explanations work well in many cases and break down in other cases. But theological naturalists cannot allow their science the latitude to incorporate nonnaturalistic explanations, or even to consider such a hypothesis. For them, science must be firmly restricted to naturalistic explanations.

This restriction of explanation leads to an unavoidable blind spot. Theological naturalism is ailing because it has no choice but to blindly pursue all problems as equals. Analyzing a nerve cell is conceptually no different from analyzing human consciousness. Explaining the ontogeny of a frog is no different from explaining the source of all life. Theological naturalism lacks the resources to look at all sides of a problem. It lacks the wisdom to know its own limitations. It is the fool that rushes in where wise men fear to tread. And it must rush in, for to do otherwise would be to deny its own convictions.

4

A God in the Machine

How did the universe and everything in it arise? In the first half of the seventeenth century René Descartes argued for purely mechanistic explanations for just about everything, including the universe. He supplied such an explanation for the sun and planets. Like corks in a whirlpool, the planets revolve about the sun in the same direction. Descartes envisioned a series of whirlpools, or vortices, to explain the formation of the solar system. The sun was at the center of an immense vortex, and smaller vortices surrounded each planet. According to Descartes, not only did the vortices explain why the planets travel around the sun, and the moons around planets, but they also explained why the planets travel in ellipses as opposed to circles.

As we saw in chapter 2, Descartes was reacting to Aristotelianism, which he argued failed to provide meaningful explanations. Fire was hot because hotness was a property of fire. In fleeing from such tautologies, Descartes sought mechanistic explanations. But would these types of explanations be guaranteed to work? What if the phenomenon in question was not amenable to a mechanistic explanation? As we saw in chapter 3, Descartes' approach would never detect this and would forever search for a solution that does not exist.

Sometimes Descartes is applauded for throwing the switch to naturalistic explanations. But this begs the question. Requiring naturalistic explanations, of how the solar system arose for example, is appropriate if the solar system arose by natural processes. But this requirement could be disastrous otherwise.

It wasn't as though Descartes had a compelling explanation. After all, his vortices were invisible. The etherlike fluid that whirled around the sun and planets could not be empirically detected. Nor did the vortices work very well in explaining the solar system we observe. Years later Isaac Newton showed why. "The hypothesis of vortices," Newton pointed out, "is utterly irreconcileable with astronomical phenomena, and rather serves to perplex than explain the heavenly motions."[1] But this would not be the end of perplexing hypotheses. The push for purely naturalistic accounts was stronger than any scientific problem. As we shall see in this chapter, religious or metaphysical arguments would continue to be used for naturalism in cosmology in spite of scientific problems.

A Rude and Ragged World

About thirty years after Descartes, the Anglican chaplain Thomas Burnet published his popular and influential *Sacred Theory of the Earth*, where he detailed the history of the earth. In the summer of 1671 Burnet toured Europe and crossed the Alps and Apennines mountain ranges. He had the experience of majesty and grandeur not uncommon for those visiting a great mountain range for the first time. But Burnet's wonder was often interrupted by the "incredible confusion" and lack of symmetry and proportion. From a distance the mountains were awe inspiring, but up close there were irregular rocks, moraines, and valleys. Maps and atlases portrayed well-ordered and symmetrical mountains, but Burnet found them to be "shapeless and ill-figured."[2]

Burnet's paradoxical observations about nature would be common-place in the coming years. Before the end of the century, the great botanist John Ray would argue on the one hand that nature revealed design but on the other hand that the world was not directly created, as evidenced by its errors and bungles. In the eighteenth century, David Hume admitted that nature's complexity made for a powerful design argument but argued that it is neutralized by the misery in the world. In the nineteenth century, Charles Darwin argued the species could not be the product of a divine creation, yet he also saw the grandeur of nature.

Mountains were not the only confusing feature of earth's geography for Burnet. Other problems included the jagged coastlines and lack of symmetry in the continents. Burnet's idealization of nature was nothing new. The Pythagoreans in ancient Greece held that the sun, moon, planets, and stars were attached to rotating spheres that produced harmonious sounds, and Plato believed the universe was designed to be simple and elegant. Two thousand years later, Johannes Kepler in the early seventeenth century sought to show how the creator designed the heavenly motions according to musical harmonics.

But the real world did not meet these idealistic expectations. The recently invented telescopes now revealed unseemly details of the moon's pockmarked surface. And with its jagged and asymmetric coastlines and mountains, the earth no doubt would also appear from afar "rude and ragged," as Burnet put it. Could we really believe these bodies were the result of a divine design?

Three centuries later, it is obvious to us that the moon's craters were created by meteorite impacts. Burnet's theological naturalism was on the mark. He called for naturalistic explanations for the moon's craters, and now we have them. But the underlying motivation was theological. The craters, it seemed to Burnet, would not have been designed by God, regardless of how they were created. Such reasoning is difficult to put to rest. As we shall see, it was soon applied to all of creation. The point here is not that theological naturalism is necessarily wrong. The point is simply that it is theological and as such is not easily overturned by empirical evidence. It was not that science was revealing naturalistic processes that were capable of creating the world. Rather, science was revealing a world that, for many, must have been created only by naturalistic processes.

Burnet's theory involved the biblical flood (which wreaked havoc and left a broken, disordered earth in its wake), but otherwise there was little resemblance between Burnet's ideas and biblical doctrine. On the other hand, Burnet was certainly no atheist, despite accusations thereof.[3] Burnet's ideas, like those of other idealists such as Kepler, were very much motivated by theism. For these thinkers, it was a concept of God, not a rejection of God, that led to their idealistic expectations.

This idealism was yet another reason that mechanistic explanations in natural history were often preferred. Toward the end of the century such elite thinkers as Edmund Halley (1656–1742) and William Whiston (1667–1752) elaborated on Burnet's idea of a naturalistic history of the earth. Halley, one of the greatest astronomers in the world, theorized that a comet was the cause of the flood. Whiston, Newton's successor at Cambridge, elaborated on Halley's idea and proposed that the earth could have been created by a comet and the flood caused by yet another comet.

On the continent the French encyclopedists held Burnet in high esteem, placing him in the company of Descartes and Newton. And G. W. Leibniz referred approvingly to Burnet's ideas. In later years the English Romantics Samuel Taylor Coleridge and William Wordsworth highly regarded Burnet.[4]

A Striking Regularity

While for some thinkers, such as Burnet, the lack of any pattern or symmetry indicated naturalism, for others the exact opposite—the *presence* of a pattern—indicated naturalism. Just as ripples in sand are caused by the action of waves, patterns in nature are suggestive of the action of natural processes.

About fifty years after Burnet wrote *Sacred Theory of the Earth*, in the early decades of the eighteenth century, one striking regularity that had not yet been explained was the clocklike workings of the solar system. Not only did all the known planets revolve about the sun in the same direction, but they did so in roughly the same plane—the sun's equatorial plane, known as the *ecliptic*. In other words, all the planets circle above the sun's equator in the same direction.

But none of these coincidences seem to be necessary. Could there be a reason that the orbits of the planets are so aligned? This was one of the questions asked at the prestigious Paris Academy, and it was answered by Daniel Bernoulli (1700–1782) in his award-winning essay of 1734.[5] Bernoulli came from a family of prominent scientists and mathematicians. His equation of fluid flow remains today an essential for university students.

Bernoulli's idea was that the sun's atmosphere was the cause of the alignment of the planet's orbits. Despite Bernoulli's genius, and the award he received, this idea failed. Not only is there no solar atmosphere extending to the planets, but even if there were it would not cause the alignment as Bernoulli described. The essay did, however, make a lasting contribution. Bernoulli devised a seemingly powerful argument that a single event or process was responsible for the alignment of the planets' orbits.

The fact that all the planets circle the sun in the ecliptic seems like a striking pattern, but no one had quantified this. Bernoulli did so by comparing the known pattern to randomly aligned orbits. Bernoulli asked the question: if the planetary orbits had fallen into place by chance, what then is the probability that they would just happen to lie in practically the same plane as they do? Bernoulli gave three different calculations, all of which showed the odds were astronomical. He picked the middle result of the three, which was that the odds of such a coincidental alignment is 1,419,856 to 1. In fact Bernoulli could have computed even longer odds by including the revolutions of the planets. The planets revolve about the sun in the same direction, and this too is a coincidence.

False Dichotomy

Bernoulli's calculation seemed to bring the power of mathematics and statistics to the argument for natural causes. The mathematics appeared to prove that a single cause or process was behind the solar system pattern. The person who would deny this, concluded Bernoulli, "must reject all the truths, which we know by induction."[6]

But the Bernoulli calculation forces an either-or decision between random chance and a mechanistic process. Bernoulli used mathematics to argue forcefully that the planets did not originate from random chance. This does not mean, however, that a single naturalistic process is our only other choice.

The solar system could, for example, be explained with a multiplicity of naturalistic causes. Indeed, as we shall see, later theories would have to resort to such a multiplicity. One reason for this is that the structure of the solar system is far richer than this simplistic dichotomy suggests. Yes, the planets orbit the sun in a common plane, but they are all different as well. Their sizes, densities, distances from the sun, orbital velocities, rate of rotation, moons, rings, and so forth are all different. Even their orbital inclinations have curious variations. There are striking patterns, but there are also many variations and differences.

A God in the Machine

There is nothing about Bernoulli's proof that restricts him to naturalistic explanations. There is no mathematical reasoning that allows Bernoulli to conclude that since the solar system is not the result of random chance, it therefore must be the result of naturalistic causes. Instead, the reasoning comes from theological naturalism. As Immanuel Kant (1724–1804) later explained, the solar system must have a naturalistic origin.

Like Burnet's theological reasoning that the earth was formed by natural processes, Kant made strong theological claims that the solar system must not have been created by God directly but rather indirectly via natural laws. In 1755 he wrote his *Allgemeine Naturgeschichte und Theorie des Himmels* (*Universal Natural History and Theory of Heaven*), where he addressed Newton's suggestion that the solar system was a divine creation.

Kant agreed that the planetary structure reveals the "sure marks of God's hand in its perfect interrelationships." And we are rightly indignant at the foolishness that ascribes "all this to chance and a lucky contingency." But Kant argued that *how* the solar system was created is a different question altogether. He argued that the solar system was created by naturalistic processes, and he presented several reasons for viewing this as conclusive.

First, why do planets revolve about the sun in the same direction? "It is clear that here there is no reason the celestial bodies must organize their orbits in one single direction." If they were arranged by "the unmediated hand of God," then we would expect them to reveal deviations and differences: "Thus, God's choice, not having the slightest motive for tying them to one single arrangement, would reveal itself with a greater freedom in all sorts of deviations and differences."[7]

And this reasoning also applies to the fact that the planetary orbits all lie in the ecliptic. Furthermore, the fact that the orbits do not precisely lie in the ecliptic also mandates a naturalistic origin: "If it was for the best that the planetary orbits were oriented on a common plane, why are they not oriented with extreme precision? And why has a portion of that deviation remained in place, when it should be avoided?"

For Kant, there must have been a natural force or process that placed the planetary orbits in the ecliptic, but not precisely via interference and interactions. It must be the mark of a natural process, for God would have aligned the orbits perfectly:

> If what the philosopher said is true, that God constantly practices geometry and if this is reflected in the methods of the general natural laws, then certainly this principle of the unmediated work of the Omnipotent

Will would be perfectly traceable and the latter would reveal in itself the perfection of geometrical precision.[8]

It is not surprising that Kant objected to the idea that nature was created by the unmediated hand of God. Those with this idea, Kant warned, "will have to make a solemn apology before the judgment seat of religion." For in this case the laws of nature bring forth nothing but "disorder and absurdity" and hence have no relation to God. What sort of God is it whose natural laws "act counter to the plan of the Divinity's wisest designs"? In this case nature obeys God only by compulsion. It has no inherent capabilities, and we are left with nothing except "a god in the machine."

Furthermore, this incapacity of nature leaves us with no position for "demonstrating the certain existence of a Highest Being." How will this, for example, counter Epicurus, who promoted a theory of atheism in ancient times? Epicurus argued that organization in nature arose from nothing more than the swerving motions of atoms. His nature had no inherent capabilities, and neither does the idea of a world that needs to be directly controlled by God. For Kant, on the other hand, matter was bound by certain necessary laws. The result is a "beautiful and orderly totality developing quite naturally out of its total dissolution and scattering. This does not happen by accident or chance."[9]

Kant argued that natural laws, left alone to their own work, "bring forth nothing but beauty and order." With a mechanistic explanation, the beauty of the world and the revelation of omnipotence are glorified in no small way. Creation by natural law glorifies God, and Kant was sure that the solar system arose via a mechanical sequence of natural laws. For Kant, these arguments demonstrated a mechanistic origin so clearly that we can entertain no doubts about it. This was proof that the solar system arose mechanistically in accordance with general natural laws.

Burnet found a lack of a pattern in the moon's craters and earth's coastlines and concluded that unguided mechanism was responsible. Bernoulli and Kant found a strong pattern in the solar system and also concluded that unguided mechanism was responsible. In both cases theological premises mandated the conclusion.

Post-Kantian Theories of the Solar System's Origin

The historical sciences were increasingly turning to mechanistic explanations involving only the laws of nature. Ironically, this was anything but a move away from religion and metaphysics, as it is often interpreted to be. Burnet, Bernoulli, and Kant's arguments could convert most empirical data into strong evidences for naturalism. If the data did not appeal to our sense of harmony, then it could not be of divine design and must have arisen naturally. If, on the other hand, the data fell into a consistent pattern, then it must be the product of a lawlike process. These were powerful arguments for naturalistic explanations, but they did not originate from scientific deduction based on empirical observations.

After Bernoulli, George Louis Leclerc, Comte de Buffon (1707–1788), and Pierre Simon Laplace, both leading scientific thinkers of the eighteenth century, proposed theories for the formation of the solar system. Buffon wrote extensively on natural history and was widely read and influential. Laplace made fundamental contributions to science and mathematics that remain important today.

Buffon and Laplace would both, in turn, make use of their own refined versions of Bernoulli's calculation. And each made successively stronger truth claims regarding their theories. Buffon replaced Bernoulli's solar atmosphere idea with a comet that collided with the sun, spewing forth solar material that would later condense to form the planets. Buffon concluded that "it is therefore extremely probable, that the planets were originally parts of the sun."[10]

Like Bernoulli's solar atmosphere idea, Buffon's comet-impact idea had its problems. How, for instance, could all the planets have such nearly circular orbits about the sun? Would they not be highly elliptical if the planetary material had emerged from the sun? Laplace replaced Buffon's idea with his Nebular Hypothesis,[11] which called for a cloud of material about the sun that rotates and condenses to form the planets.

It was, claimed Laplace, the "true system of the world."[12] But despite the great mathematician's confidence, the Nebular Hypothesis had its problems. For example, there was a growing list of exceptions to the striking regularity that initially had fueled Bernoulli's calculation. The moons of Uranus and Saturn did not all fit the pattern. Nor of course did comets. Why were the planetary orbits slightly inclined at odd angles rather than precisely aligned with the sun's equator, and why were the orbits not more circular? Likewise, why do the planets spin at odd angles, and why don't their densities reveal a pattern?

Laplace's great confidence that his theory was true ultimately came from his great confidence that the solar system had a natural origin. Hadn't Bernoulli's calculation proved that? And Laplace's versions of that calculation reinforced this conclusion. The Nebular Hypothesis may have had its problems, but it was the best naturalistic explanation, and the explanation must be naturalistic. As for the anomalies, Laplace viewed them as remarkable instances of "the great variety that takes place among the movements of the heavenly bodies."[13]

In the nineteenth century, the idea that the solar system originated as the result of naturalistic processes became increasingly accepted. It was not the Nebular Hypothesis that was taken as fact so much as naturalism itself. The Nebular Hypothesis could be replaced by another naturalistic description if need be. Bernoulli, Buffon, Laplace, and later cosmologists could disagree on the particular explanation, but the common thread was that the explanation must be naturalistic.

The fact of the solar system's naturalistic evolution was not sealed by an empirically based, scientifically deduced, compelling explanation where all the evidential pieces clearly fell into place. Indeed, the different explanations made mutually exclusive claims about how the solar system originated, and each failed at one point or another to explain the empirical data.

All of this leads to the curious combination of metaphysical certainty and scientific ambiguity in the historical sciences. On the one hand naturalism is a fact, while on the other hand the theories themselves contain all manner of problems. On the one hand scientists seem to be proposing useful fiction—theories merely intended to serve as explanatory devices—yet on the other hand they routinely claim their theories are true, or approximately true with only a few details left to be worked out.

Twentieth-Century Theories

In Laplace's Nebular Hypothesis, planet formation is a natural consequence of star formation. In Buffon's comet theory, planet formation is a separate event and not a consequence of star formation. This fundamental difference defines the two categories of theories for the origin of the solar system—the monistic and dualistic theories, respectively. Monistic theories, such as Laplace's Nebular Hypothesis, hold that all the major components of the solar system formed together. Dualistic theories, such as Buffon's comet theory of planet formation, hold that stars form by one process and planets form by a different process.

As the twentieth century began, the mounting problems with the Nebular Hypothesis caused a reevaluation and search for alternate explanations. A major problem was that the sun rotates too slowly. The vast majority of the angular momentum in the solar system resides in the planets, a fact that was difficult to reconcile with the Nebular Hypothesis.

And so the twentieth century witnessed a series of monistic and dualistic theories competing to explain the solar system's origin. There was the dualistic theory of a close encounter with a nearby star, proposed by Thomas Chamberlin and Forest Moulton and later by James Jeans and Harold Jeffreys. But such a close encounter could not reproduce the high angular momentum we observe in the planetary orbits. Also, material ripped from the sun by the encounter would be too hot to condense and form planets.

Henry Russell proposed a new monistic theory calling for a rise in density of the collapsing solar nebula. Also, the idea of magnetic braking was considered as a mechanism for depleting the sun's angular momentum. This was followed by the dualistic theory of Hannes Alfvén and Otto Schmidt and then the monistic theory of Gerard Kuiper and Harold Urey. Schmidt's dualistic theory was later refined in the Safronov-Wetherill model, and after this A. G. W. Cameron promoted the "supernova trigger" hypothesis.[14]

Both monistic and dualistic theories were repeatedly proposed throughout the twentieth century. In fact, as historian Stephen Brush observes, the time scale for reversing the answer has grown shorter and shorter as we approach the present. Hence the origin of the solar system, says Brush, is an unsolved problem.[15]

Today's Hypothesis and Problems

Today's accepted theory for the origin of the solar system is a variation of the Nebular Hypothesis. It goes something like this. A large cloud of material, including dust, hydrogen, and helium, collapses to form the sun and a surrounding disk. The rotational rate increases as the cloud collapses. It also heats up, especially in the inner region, say within the orbit of Jupiter. In this inner region, only rocky materials can withstand the high temperatures, and they collect to form the inner planets, initially as molten blobs. Later they are coated with particles that collect on their surface. These become the crusts of the inner planets.

Between Mars and Jupiter there is no planet; instead we find the asteroid belt. This is because Jupiter perturbed the nascent planets that formed in that region, causing them to collide rather than coalesce. The result is a ring of asteroids, rather than a planet, circling the sun.

In the outer regions of the solar system, where the temperature is lower, icy dust collects to form small planetesimals that later attract the hydrogen and helium gases. Leftover planetesimals may be captured as moons or are ejected to the outer reaches of the solar system to become comets. Hence the composition of comets and meteorites should represent the early solar nebula. Later, the sun's radiation and solar wind drive any remaining gas out of the solar system, and the sun's rotation is dramatically slowed by magnetic braking.

This is our modern, complicated rendition of Laplace's Nebular Hypothesis, and there yet remain several anomalies to explain. For instance, Venus and Uranus have anomalous spin characteristics. Also, about a third of the more than one hundred moons in the solar system have irregular orbits, revolving about their host planet in the wrong direction or revolving faster than their host planet spins. This would not occur if they were formed by a condensing cloud. Also, Pluto's orbit is more elliptical than that of the other planets and significantly inclined from the ecliptic.

There is no general explanation for these many anomalies. It could be that huge impacts reversed the spin of Venus and tipped Uranus on its side. Perhaps moons that revolve too fast have dropped from a higher orbit and thus increased their rate of rotation. Or they may have been captured by rather than formed with the planet.

As for Pluto, one idea is that a large planetesimal passed near Neptune, lost some energy, and fell down near Jupiter, which ejected it to beyond Pluto. In the process the orbits of Jupiter, Saturn, Uranus, and Neptune were all perturbed, and Neptune, in turn, perturbed Pluto into the highly eccentric and inclined orbit we observe today.

Another difficulty with today's theory of the solar system origin is the great size of the outer gaseous planets. In order to accumulate so much light gas, they must have formed very quickly, because early on the sun's solar wind would have blown the gas out of the solar system altogether.

One explanation for this is that these planets formed via a faster-acting mechanism known as *disk instability*. But if this works for Jupiter and

Saturn, it leaves open the question of why Uranus and Neptune are not so large. If the disk instability mechanism gave Jupiter and Saturn their thick atmospheres, why didn't it give thick atmospheres to Uranus and Neptune?

One answer is that our solar system formed in a cluster of stars. Perhaps the neighboring stars were so close that radiation heated the gases in the outer reaches of our solar system, making the gases more difficult for Uranus and Neptune to capture.[16]

Yet another problem with today's theory of the solar system's origin comes from recent discoveries of planets revolving about distant stars. These extrasolar planetary systems do not fit contemporary theories, as we are repeatedly discovering huge Jupiter-size and larger gaseous planets that orbit their sun at a distance that would be inside the orbit of Mercury in our own system. The orbits are often highly elliptical and like nothing that our theories would predict. In an extreme case, a planet has been found in a triple-star system. The planet is closer to the central star than are the other two stars. It is a planet that "should not exist."[17] As one researcher put it, "These discoveries are making it very difficult to stick to the party line endorsing the so-called standard model."[18]

A Complicated Universe

The formation of the solar system is not the only problem in cosmology that is not easily described as a product of natural history. The origin of the moon, for instance, has undergone a range of diverse theories. Most other moons in the solar system are a tiny fraction the size of the planet they orbit, but the earth-moon system is more like a double planet system.

If the solar system arose via the Nebular Hypothesis, then we might think the moon, like a celestial sister, condensed from material spun off from the earth as it too was condensing. This is the coaccretion hypothesis. But how would this process create such a large, low-density moon?

An alternate explanation is that the moon was ejected from the earth. This fission hypothesis helps explain the observation that the moon is slowing in its orbit, but difficulties arise with angular momentum and tidal forces. A third explanation is that the moon formed elsewhere and was captured into earth's orbit. This capture hypothesis has difficulties explaining chemical similarities between the earth and moon and the moon's nearly circular orbit.

Different variations and combinations of these ideas were attempted in the twentieth century, but all had difficulties. This led to the giant-impact hypothesis, where a Mars-sized object collides with earth and rocky debris was ejected, some of which remained in earth orbit and aggregated into the moon.

One problem is that the giant-impact hypothesis works best if the Mars-sized impactor does not come from remote regions of the solar system but from roughly the same orbit as earth. But how could this happen? One solution is that the impactor formed in one of the two stable Lagrange points in the sun-earth system. These two points are the same distance from the sun, 60 degrees behind and ahead of the earth. Perhaps the impactor condensed at one of these points. In other words, earth and the impactor formed in different places in the same orbit. Then later the impactor was perturbed and so eventually collided with earth, causing the formation of the moon.[19]

Like the origin of the solar system, the origin of the moon has required a complex explanation with a series of contingent events producing the final result. Problems remain, but presumably they can be addressed with additional contingent events occurring at the appropriate times and locations.

On a larger scale, galaxies also pose confusions. They are thought to arise through an evolutionary process: in the early stages, smaller collections of stars form as large gas clouds collapse, and in later stages, encounters, collisions, and mergers produce the more mature, larger galaxies. But in the past few years, large, mature galaxies have been observed in the far reaches of the universe. These galaxies are so distant that we are observing them when the universe was young. How did these mature galaxies form so early in the universe? Similarly, galaxies appear in clusters, and recently a faint distant galaxy cluster, from the early stages of the universe, was also found to be mature. How these structures evolved so quickly remains unknown. These results would have been considered impossible ten years ago.[20]

Many galaxies also have peculiar rotations. Stars orbit the galaxies' central core faster than we would expect. If these galaxies evolved this way, then there must be an unknown force holding them together. One explanation is that there must be invisible *dark* matter surrounding the galaxy that causes the higher orbital speeds of the outer stars.

These are but a sampling of the unexplained phenomena in the cosmos. Three hundred years ago Isaac Newton explained planetary motion with an elegant formulation. All of the various motions were explained as the result of natural laws. Since then, cosmologists have tried to explain how our universe and its contents arose via an equally simple naturalistic description. The results have been decidedly mixed. Explanations tend to be short lived, and they certainly are not elegant or simple. As one researcher puts it, "The universe is always more complicated than our cosmological theories would have it."[21]

The universe is supposed to be the product of nothing more than blind natural laws, yet it is so complicated. Why is it so difficult for us to understand what a mindless process created? Perhaps, as one cosmologist speculated, any universe that is simple enough to be understood is too simple to produce a mind able to understand it.[22] This idea is known as the *anthropic principle*. In order for complex, intelligent life to arise in a universe, that universe must have a particular property (in this case complexity). Since humans exist, our universe must have that property. If it did not, then we would not be here to observe the universe in the first place. Thus, the only universes that could ever be observed and analyzed are complex universes.

Of course this is speculation, and it is not the only case of such reasoning in cosmology. For several decades now, scientists have observed that our universe appears to be not only complex but rigged for life. A variety of conditions and laws of nature are just right to support the existence of everything from atoms to stars. The mass of the electron, the strength of gravity, and a host of other natural constants are finely tuned in our favor.

How could this be? Did the fabric of nature just happen to be tuned so life would work? There seems to be no physical or naturalistic rationale for this incredible set of coincidences. Cosmologists have responded with the theory that there exist a huge number of trial runs, in the form of parallel universes (or perhaps different regions within our universe). In these multiple universes, or *multiverse*, the rules of nature are varied over a tremendous range of possibilities. And according to the anthropic principle, the only trial runs that produce intelligent observers are those that are tuned just right. We should not be amazed that our universe appears finely tuned, for it is only in such a universe that intelligent life would arise and be capable of observing the universe.

The universe's fine-tuning seems quite peculiar, but theological naturalism mandates a naturalistic explanation. The multiverse hypothesis provides such an explanation. For some cosmologists, multiverses make the fine-tuning seem "much less miraculous."[23] The multiverse hypothesis is another example of science's blind spot. The historical sciences are constrained to mechanistic explanations, even if this leads to untestable or unprovable hypotheses. We may never find a parallel universe, but that doesn't mean they aren't out there. As one research paper on this subject concluded, the multiverse hypothesis "remains a matter of faith rather than of proof."[24]

But such frank assessments are rare. Yes, the multiverse hypothesis is a matter of faith, especially when viewed as another project within a theological naturalism that is based on religious assumptions. But this context is rarely understood. Instead, naturalistic origins are typically reported to be a fact, though the details have yet to be worked out. The multiverse hypothesis, explained a 2003 *Scientific American* issue, is now a fact. The cover of that issue declared, "Infinite Earths in Parallel Universes Really Exist."[25]

The problem here is not so much that theological naturalism has failed. The problem is that our assessment of naturalism has failed. There is nothing wrong with pursuing naturalistic explanations in cosmology.

But those committed to naturalistic explanations, like those committed to supernaturalistic explanations, can always devise a theory to explain what we observe. Like supernaturalism, naturalism can never be judged a failure, for there is no test for failure. Failed hypotheses simply lead to more complex hypotheses. Unfortunately, the question of origins within cosmology is too often dominated by these extremes. Either the cosmos evolved completely naturally with no detectable divine action or design, or the cosmos was created with no history. Each extreme rejects the other as unacceptable and, as well, rejects intermediate views. As we have seen, theological naturalism rejects the possibility of detectable design, even design involving strictly natural causes. Yes, we need to pursue naturalistic explanations in cosmology, but we need to understand that there are theological motives behind this pursuit.

5

Nature's Innovative Power

Theological naturalism in the seventeenth and eighteenth centuries was not restricted to theories of the origins of the cosmos, it also influenced thinking about the origins of the species. As we saw in chapter 2, early in the eighteenth century the great botanist John Ray, influenced by the Cambridge Platonists, called for an indirect creation of the species. A few years later Benoit De Maillet (1656–1738) imagined how life might have arisen. Borrowing from Descartes's notion of vortices, De Maillet proposed the idea of an evolving universe over billions of years. After the earth coalesced, the seeds of life found favorable conditions within the oceans. Plants in the ocean evolved and gave rise to land plants. Likewise, fish evolved and gave rise to birds and terrestrial animals.[1]

Later in the century such speculation on how the universe and life arose naturalistically continued. Comte de Buffon considered the idea of common descent, and he influenced such men as Étienne Geoffroy St. Hilaire (1772–1844) and Jean-Baptiste Lamarck (1744–1829). It was Lamarck who promoted the idea of evolution by the law of inheritance of acquired characteristics. Lamarck's belief in this version of evolution of the species was uncompromising, though it would later be thoroughly rejected.

Lamarck's theological concern was with extinctions. He was a sort of deist, and he believed that nature must exhibit harmony. Catastrophes and extinctions were unacceptable. Lamarck avoided extinctions by having the ancient fossil species evolve to produce today's species.[2] It was another example of theological naturalism, and today's evolutionists can only wonder how Lamarck was so convinced of his theory of evolution.[3] After all, he lacked what evolutionists view as Darwin's crucial insights.

As with theories of the solar system's origin, the commitment to naturalistic explanations for the origin of species did not arise merely from empirical evidence. Lamarck's theological concerns required a naturalistic explanation. And although Lamarck's theory was harshly criticized by many, it did provide a purely naturalistic explanation, with at least some level of detail for the origin of species. Some of Darwin's early influences, such as Robert Edmond Grant, advocated Lamarck's ideas.[4] As Darwin later wrote, Lamarck performed the "eminent service of arousing attention to the probability of all changes in the organic, as well as in the inorganic world, being the result of law, and not of miraculous interposition."[5] But that probability was arrived at by Lamarck's rationalism with its theological premises, rather than via empiricism.

Darwin's own grandfather, Erasmus Darwin, argued for the mutability of species in his 1794 book *Zoonomia*. And in the nineteenth century Auguste Comte (1798–1857) described how natural selection could have evolved the species:

> If one concedes that all possible organisms were successively placed during a suitable time in all imaginable environments, most of these organisms would necessarily end by disappearing, thus leaving alive only those that could satisfy the general laws of that fundamental equilibrium: it is probably through a succession of analogous eliminations that the biological harmony was established little by little on our planet, where indeed we still see it modifying itself unceasingly in a similar manner.[6]

In 1844 Robert Chambers anonymously published *Vestiges of the Natural History of Creation*. This best-selling volume was steeped in theological naturalism. Surely it was ridiculous, wrote Chambers, to expect a deity "to interfere personally and specially on every occasion when a new shell-fish or reptile was to be ushered into existence."[7]

Finally, in the mid-nineteenth century Charles Darwin developed his theory of evolution. And half a world away, naturalist Alfred Russel Wallace produced a solution that was strikingly similar to Darwin's theory of evolution. Even Wallace's language was similar.[8] Wallace and Darwin had developed their respective theories independently, but of course they were working under a similar cultural influence. As we shall see in chapter 8, Darwin had many theological concerns that his theory of evolution resolved. He had no idea how biology's complexities could have arisen,[9] but he knew they must have arisen naturally. As one historian put it, both Wallace and Darwin believed in transmutation, and so they sought a suitable mechanism.[10]

What Kant and Laplace had done for cosmology Wallace and Darwin did for the origin of species. Science now had theories that provided a framework for research yet were sufficiently open ended so as to be adaptable to a wide range of findings. The species, according to Darwin, arose primarily from natural selection acting on naturally occurring biological variation. Natural selection was not really a new natural law. It was merely a consequence of biological variation in a competitive environment. Those designs that work better will produce more offspring.

The Random Design Null Hypothesis

This is how evolution was supposed to work. But did it make sense? After all, anyone familiar with animal husbandry knew of the limits encountered with breeding techniques. One could breed for certain traits, but only to an extent. Likewise, fossils made abrupt appearances in the geological strata and then persisted unchanged. And of course, life was overwhelmingly complex. Could it really arise on its own?

The answer here was the same as that given in cosmology. Theological naturalism mandated mechanistic explanations for the heavens, and it also mandated mechanistic explanations for the species. Burnet had argued that the world's lack of beauty and symmetry was evidence against a divine design. So too, Darwin argued that a range of biological data were evidence against divine creation.

"Why should similar bones have been created to form the wing and the leg of a bat, used as they are for such totally different purposes, namely flying and walking?"[11] Darwin rhetorically asked. Darwin could not actually explain how the wing or leg of a bat could have arisen, but he knew how they *could not* have arisen. As we shall see in chapter 8, Darwin found this and many other examples in biology to be inexplicable on the theory of creation.

Likewise, just as Kant argued the pattern of the solar system could not have been created, so too Darwin argued the pattern of the species could not have been created. Kant argued that whereas the planets all traveled in the same direction and roughly in the same plane (the ecliptic), a creator would have had no such restriction and would have placed the planets in random orbits. This idea of a random design as the null hypothesis was inherent in Bernoulli's 1734 probability calculation, where he argued there must be a single natural cause for the planet's orbits.

Like the planets, the species fall into a distinct pattern. Though complicated and with many exceptions, they generally have been thought to fall into a nested hierarchy where the species divide into a few distinct clusters. Within these clusters one finds yet more lower-level clusters, and so on. This, Darwin explained, would not be the case if the species had been created: "The several subordinate groups in any class cannot be ranked in a single file, but seem clustered round points, and these round other points, and so on in almost endless cycles. If species had been independently created, no explanation would have been possible of this kind of classification."[12]

This notion that created species ought to be randomly designed remains important today in evolutionary theory. Terms such as "created independently" carry the inherent assumption of random design, which is the basis of evolution's null hypothesis. Evolutionists explain that design patterns between the species prove that they do not have independent origin.

Evolution may struggle to explain how the species could have evolved and how the details of the pattern could have arose. But these are mere research questions, for, they claim, evolution must be the cause one way or another. Bernoulli's argument and probability calculation later became tainted by the various exceptions and anomalies to the pattern. When William Herschel (1738–1822) announced that the moons of Uranus have retrograde orbits, Laplace remained unmoved, for it was merely a research problem. His Nebular Hypothesis was unharmed. These retrograde orbits could be explained as anomalies resulting from historical contingencies. Bernoulli's clocklike solar system was becoming a patchwork of motion. Likewise, the biological patterns Darwin thought mandated naturalism would later require far more complicated explanations.

The Predictions of Evolution

According to Darwinists, the theory of evolution is so obvious and compelling that it should be considered to be a fact rather than a theory. Just as gravity and the roundness of the earth are facts, so too evolution is a fact. As Darwinists explain, there really is no counterevidence. Everything in biology is what we would expect if evolution were true. Evolution's predictions, they claim, have all come true.

But successful predictions do not necessarily make for successful theories. Two thousand years ago Ptolemy developed a theory describing how the moon, sun, planets, and stars moved, assuming the earth was at the center of all this motion. Ptolemy's geocentric model was quite accurate. It successfully predicted celestial motion, including the retrograde motion of Mars, for example. It successfully predicted eclipses. It had many successful predictions—and it was wrong.

Clearly, successful predictions, even if very impressive, do not prove theories to be true. In fact successful predictions can come from theories that are known to be false. Using successful predictions to evaluate the veracity of a theory requires a good deal of care. But evolutionists routinely claim that successful predictions have proven evolution. Science writer Carl Zimmer, for example, writes that similar genes doing similar jobs in different species "must have a common ancestry."[13] Scientist Sean Carroll claims that there is "only one inescapable conclusion" for such genetic similarities: common ancestry.[14] In their biology textbook Stephen Stearns and Rolf Hoekstra inform the student that similar genes found in different species "establish shared descent from common ancestors."[15]

Science is more than merely tallying up predictions. Ptolemy's geocentric model is a classic example of how a long list of correct predictions can be made by a theory that is entirely wrong. In fact, the idea that an evidence proves a theory is a logical fallacy known as affirming the consequent. So we need to be careful when using predictions to evaluate the truth value of a theory. But there is another problem altogether: the tendency for proponents to exaggerate the success of their theory.

A Theory without an Explanation

It seems inevitable that scientific theories, evolution included, encounter predictions gone wrong. According to the rules of logic, such difficulties falsify the theory. That is, if a theory makes a prediction that is later discovered to be false, then the theory itself is false. This is simple common sense. If my theory predicts a solar eclipse tomorrow, and the eclipse fails to occur, then the theory is wrong.

But science is rarely so straightforward, for few theories are so rigid or specific. If a false prediction is discovered, then the theory can be adjusted to account for the new information. For instance, Ptolemy's geocentric model contained many epicycles describing the celestial motion. Adding more "epicycles" circumvents the necessity of disposing of an idea altogether.

In some instances, adjustments made to scientific ideas are quite reasonable. Our understanding of physics, for instance, was adjusted when relativity and quantum mechanics came along in the twentieth century. It was found that while Newtonian physics works fine for large objects at slow speeds, it breaks down for small particles and relativistic speeds near the speed of light. So Newtonian physics was understood to have limited applicability. But there is no need to entirely reject Newtonian physics merely because it makes false predictions when dealing with certain types of problems.

On the other hand, sometimes the adjustments made to scientific ideas become excessive. Ptolemy's geocentric model ended up requiring a great many epicycles. While this technique could describe many celestial motions, such complexity in a model appears more as a data-fitting exercise than as a true description of the problem at hand.

The problem with evolution is not that there are a few minor false predictions that can be fixed with some adjustments to the theory. The problem is that evolution has a great many fundamental predictions gone wrong. For instance, one of the most basic and fundamental predictions of evolution is that *there exist evolutionary mechanisms that are capable of producing the species.* But after the better part of two centuries of research, these still remain undiscovered.

How is it that the millions upon millions of different species, with all of their unique designs, arose? The answer often given is this occurs via natural selection. Hence evolutionists often describe natural selection as having a sort of creative capability. But this is misleading, as natural selection never designed anything. All natural selection does is kill off the ill-suited designs—evolution's failed experiments. Failed designs do not survive, and only the good designs reproduce. The question remains: how did those mind-boggling designs arise in the first place? One problem here is that the biological design space is enormous and filled mostly with useless, nonfunctional designs. How does evolution create the rare gems—the functional and successful designs that then can be selected for? As has been pointed out, "The origin of species—Darwin's problem—remains unsolved."[16]

This problem is further aggravated by the failure of another prediction: that *biological variation occurs naturally*. In Darwin's theory, natural selection preserves those biological variations that are more fit. Darwin well understood that in a given population there is variation. There are the taller and the shorter, the heavier and the lighter, the faster and the slower, and so forth. Natural selection, according to evolutionists, tends to select those individuals with the best overall combination for reproduction. But from where did this variation come? This, according to evolution, is something that naturally arises in replicating life forms. It is, in a sense, "free" as far as evolution is concerned.

But today we have a better understanding than Darwin did about how this variation arises, and it is anything but free. Biological variation arises from the complex molecular machinery within the cell. In the nineteenth century Gregor Mendel (1822–1884) discovered the foundation of modern genetics, and the twentieth century filled in the details. We now know that the molecular mechanisms that produce genetic variation are incredibly complex. Whereas early evolutionists might have envisioned a simple sort of random perturbing force, we now have discovered a highly intricate Mendelian machine behind variation. From where did this mechanism for variation come?

Darwinists claim that evolution created this machine. In other words, evolution is supposed to have produced a fine-tuned machine that is, in turn, supposed to be the engine for evolution itself. This is circular, for without variation, natural selection is powerless to work. Yet natural selection is supposed to have created just what it needed—a wonderful source of variation. Biological variation does not occur naturally, it occurs via an intricate machine.

In fact, not only is variation produced by a fine-tuned machine, but that machine is actually geared for successful adaptation. For example, when a population of bacteria is subjected to harsh conditions, they tend to increase their mutation rate. It is as though a signal has been sent saying, "It is time to adapt." Also, a small fraction of the population increases its mutation rates even higher yet. These *hypermutators* ensure that an even greater variety of adaptive change is explored. And the mutations themselves do not appear randomly throughout the genome but are concentrated in certain areas that can produce helpful changes. In other words, pathways of adaptation are, to a certain extent, already laid out.

These findings are leading to new research in antibiotics. In recent years a dangerous situation has arisen: antibiotics have been rendered less effective as harmful bacteria evolve resistance to them. A new strategy to enhance the effectiveness of antibiotics involves interfering with the protein that promotes mutations in harmful bacteria. This research uses the fact that bacteria adapt via a complex design rather than a simple evolutionary mechanism.

All of this is awkward for evolution. Instead of single mutations leading to a new functionality one step at a time, we must believe that evolution first produced this marvelous adaptation machine. Organisms, Darwinists must say, have evolved the capability to respond to environmental challenges. But how did that happen? Mutational rates are able to speed up when needed and concentrate in those locations where needed, as evolution anticipates the need for future adaptation.

The problem of how evolution could have produced the species is yet further aggravated by the failure to identify how adaptive changes can produce the large-scale change evolution requires. Evolution predicts that this *adaptive change should eventually add up to macroevolution*. But this is yet another prediction that we do not observe in biology. Not only are adaptive changes the result of a complex variation machine, but they also do not show evidence of extrapolating to greater changes, such as changing the overall body plan. Some evolutionists have given up on this idea and instead think that macroevolution must be caused by some other mechanism.[17] Macroevolution, as one evolutionist put it, is more than repeated rounds of microevolution.[18]

The fact that there seems to be a barrier to large-scale evolutionary change was evident in Darwin's day. Breeders were well aware that while animal husbandry could induce significant changes, such changes nonetheless appeared to have their limits. Today nothing has changed. Cows can be bred for greater milk production, wheat for more grain production, corn for more oil production, but of course they remain cows, wheat, and corn.

These findings indicate that contrary to evolution's prediction, adaptive change does not appear to add up to macroevolution. If anything, what the plethora of experimentation tells us is that there appear to be limits and resistance to change. These findings also cast doubt upon another prediction of evolution, namely, that *species do not resist genetic change.*

This increasingly appears to be yet another flawed Darwinian prediction. At the very least we must admit we do not understand how such a view could be true. Macroevolution calls for massive genotype changes. But post-Darwinian findings are quite the opposite of this prediction. Rather than species' exhibiting fluidity, they seem to resist change and exhibit stasis (as is observed in the fossil record). Geneticist I. M. Lerner coined the term *genetic homeostasis* to describe this general finding, for it has been known for decades that organisms tend to *resist* genetic change.[19]

The problems we have looked at so far deal with the mechanism of evolution. Predictions based on how evolution is supposed to work by and large have failed. Evolutionists consider these failures to be research problems. These predictions are viewed not as being false but rather as not yet understood. This is, of course, understandable. One can hardly expect proponents of a theory to admit things are going wrong. Instead, they appeal to future research as holding the answers to these riddles. But in some cases even this explanation becomes strained.

When a Prediction Is Not Really a Prediction

One prediction states that *the fundamental molecular processes within the cell, that perform functions common to all life, originate from a common ancestor.* In other words, processes that are found in all species must have been present in the common ancestor of all the species. And one such fundamental process is the replication of the DNA molecule.

DNA replication is a common and central feature of all known cellular life. Cells are the basic unit of life, and to replicate themselves they make a copy of the DNA they contain. The DNA consists of pairs of long molecular strands, and a small army of proteins performs a series of fascinating and complex tasks to make a copy of each pair of strands.

This process is essentially the same in all species. For instance, at designated starting points, the strands are separated, and each strand then serves as a template upon which a new copy of the other, complementary strand is synthesized. In the end, the result is two pairs of strands where originally there was just one pair.

One intriguing aspect of this operation is that the synthesis is performed in the opposite direction on each strand. That is, as the strands are unzipped a Y is formed. On one of the single strands, the proteins synthesize a new strand continuously as the original DNA strands are unzipped. This way, as more strand becomes exposed, it quickly is covered with its new paired strand. On the other single strand, however, the proteins synthesize a new strand in the opposite direction, away from the unzipping action. This makes sense because paired DNA strands are chemically antiparallel. But it makes for a complex process. As the strand is exposed due to unzipping, the proteins start close to the intersection of the Y, at the location that has most recently been exposed. The proteins then move *away* from the intersection as they synthesize a new paired strand. At some point the proteins halt, move back toward the intersection of the Y, and begin the process again on the newly exposed section of strand. Hence on one of the strands replication is continuous (the "leading" strand), and on the other strand replication is discontinuous (the "lagging" strand).

There is of course a great deal more detail to this process. For our purposes, what is important is that this complex and somewhat devious process is found in all cellular life. It is a classic example of the type of fundamental molecular processes that evolution predicts to originate in a common ancestor. How could it evolve twice? But according to some evolutionists, it appears this is exactly what happened, for too many of the key proteins are too different in the various species to be related via common descent.[20]

The response of evolutionists to this finding is to drop the prediction and modify evolution. Now they say that some fundamental molecular processes within the cell, processes that perform functions common to all life, perhaps did not originate from a common ancestor but rather may evolve independently.

Hence the prediction was never really a prediction after all. The direct opposite of the prediction is what was suggested by the research, and evolution is simply expanded to accommodate this new finding. The theory became more complicated as it now must account for unexpected and seemingly contradictory findings.

This is not an isolated example. Consider the many examples of closely related species that have some surprising differences. According to evolution, similar species must share a relatively recent common ancestor. *Rana fusca* of Southeast Asia and *Rana esculents* of Central Europe are two similar frog species. For the vast majority of evolutionary history, these two species are to have shared a common lineage. Their common ancestor would have been a frog with a long evolutionary history behind it. A small single-cell organism evolved into a multicellular creature, leading to fish, then to amphibians, and finally to the ancestral frog with all the characteristic features that make it a frog. After all this common history, the lineage produces *Rana fusca* and *Rana esculents*.

The eyes of *Rana fusca* and *Rana esculents* are, not surprisingly, quite similar and naturally are thought to be directly inherited from their common ancestor. Therefore they would be expected to derive from the same genes and the same embryonic development pathway. In other words, evolution predicts that *similar structures in cousin species should derive from similar genes and embryonic development*. Indeed, it is fundamental to evolution that similarities in different species, inherited via common descent, share similar genes and development pathways. One 2004 textbook notes an example of this as a key evidence for evolution.[21]

What the textbook fails to acknowledge and inform the student of is that this is *not* generally the case. It is a prediction that has now been dropped, for the data do not support it. In our frog example, *Rana fusca* develops the lens from the epidermis on the optic cup. The optic cup induces the epidermis to differentiate into the lens, which ends up perfectly fitting. It makes sense that the lens perfectly fits in the optic cup, since it is developing from the epidermis. *Rana esculents*, however, develops the lens without the presence of the optic cup. In one case the optic cup is the inducer, in the other case the optic cup is irrelevant—it can be completely cut out. As Gavin de Beer puts it, the lenses in these two closely related species "differ completely in the mechanism by which determination and differentiation are brought about. This is no isolated example."[22]

Indeed it is not an isolated example. Not in the development of eyes, and not in a great many other structures as well.[23] As de Beer writes:

> It is now clear that the pride with which it was assumed that the inheritance of homologous structures from a common ancestor explained homology was misplaced; for such inheritance cannot be ascribed to identity of genes. . . . What mechanism can it be that results in the production of homologous organs, the same "patterns," in spite of their not being controlled by the same genes? I asked this question in 1938, and it has not been answered.[24]

Examples of this continue to be discovered,[25] and they make for awkward evidence. Evolution's prediction is falsified, and we now must believe that although similar structures in similar species are preserved in the adult stage, their genetic and embryonic development is somehow changed around to something completely different. Different genes can create the conserved structure via a different development process. This will, as one researcher put it, "please anyone who admires nature's innovative power."[26]

6

When Predictions Go Wrong

When Charles Darwin first developed the details of evolutionary theory, he worked mostly alone. Setting forth a new paradigm for biology was a big job that he knew he could not complete to the skeptic's satisfaction. So while he did his best to present details and thorough arguments, he also asked for the reader's indulgence. "This abstract, which I now publish," explained Darwin in the introduction to *On the Origin of Species*, "must necessarily be imperfect." Hostile readers would exploit a single error if they could find one, or complain about deficiencies. Darwin, anticipating such criticism, asked for a charitable reading. No doubt errors had crept in, though he was always cautious.

Furthermore, Darwin knew that much more supporting work would be necessary, as "scarcely a single point is discussed in this volume on which facts cannot be adduced, often apparently leading to conclusions directly opposite to those at which I have arrived." He concluded with a simple request for a fair hearing: "A fair result can be obtained only by fully stating and balancing the facts and arguments on both sides of each question; and this is here impossible."[1]

While Darwin may have been incapable of fully exploring his new hypothesis, now, a century and a half later, we can say the job has been completed. It would be difficult to even guess how many scientists and research projects have now examined evolutionary theory from every angle. The results are in. As we saw in chapter 5, many of the fundamental predictions of evolution were challenged by twentieth-century biology. In this chapter, we continue to explore the many important evolutionary predictions that are problematic.

Patching Up Predictions

Because the design space in biology is enormous, *different lineages evolving independently for millions of years are not expected to arrive at the same intricate design*. This is because Darwin's theory denies any final causes. Biology must follow blind, unguided processes that have no particular end in sight. It is an open-loop process that meanders through an astronomical design space influenced only by the unguided events of the moment. Given the enormous size of that design space, it is unlikely that evolution would arrive at a similar design in independent lineages, in different environments, and starting from different initial conditions.

Indeed, one of the strong evidences cited *for* common descent are the similar designs found in not-so-distant species. There is no apparent reason for that design, so it must be a remnant of common descent—an unpredictable result of the contingencies of naturalistic processes. It couldn't have evolved independently in multiple lineages. Instead, the design must have arisen once in a common ancestor and then persisted in later species.

But what happens when similar designs are discovered in distant species, so distant that a common ancestor cannot be used to explain their origin? What happens when common solutions are found in species that, even according to evolution, are widely divergent? These cases are unexpected surprises to evolutionists, for they contradict evolution's prediction that biology is beholden to a contingent process.

The inevitable explanation is that natural selection converged on the same solution twice. Biology's design space may be huge, but these repeated solutions, for some reason, were evolved independently. Perhaps the environments were sufficiently similar so as to mandate the same design. Or perhaps other competing designs were few and far between. These explanations are sometimes given, but they rarely work. In evolution, similar environments do not cause similar designs to be created. Similar designs must have been created independently by evolution's unguided process. Furthermore, there are too many known examples where similar designs appear in distant species, *in spite of* different environments and in spite of the availability of competing designs.

There is the marsupial-placental convergence, where, aside from the reproductive organs, one finds uncanny similarities amongst a wide diversity of creatures. Over and over within the marsupials and placentals, similar designs arise. Everything from rats, cats, and mice to anteaters, flying squirrels, and wolves shows up twice in these cousin mammalian lineages.

Then there are the succulent plants of the southern African deserts that are repeats of the various designs found in the western hemisphere. Or again, if you see a pink, long-legged wading bird with the head, plumage, and shape of the beautiful flamingo, you may actually be looking at a roseate spoonbill.[2] Intricate spider-web designs are also repeated, even down to number of spokes and the lengths and densities of the spiral design that captures bugs. It is a remarkable example of convergence of a complex behavior where a great many other behaviors would be possible.[3]

Then there is the convergence of the eye in, for example, humans and squids. Different initial conditions and different environments led to a similar intricate design. There are many more examples.[4] How does evolution work through the vast expanse of biological possibilities and yet repeatedly converge at the same design? We don't exactly know, but we do know that another evolutionary prediction has problems.

How can evolutionists incorporate this into their scheme? The answer that evolutionists are left with is that contingency rules, except when it doesn't rule. Similar designs found in not-so-distant species are assumed to be due to contingency; on the other hand, similar designs in distant species are assumed not to be due to contingency. In those cases selection is supposed to have caused convergent designs to come forth. One way or another, whatever we find in biology is ascribed to evolution.

Another prediction that is in need of revision is that *evolution results in a pattern of common descent.* This is the idea that the different species are ultimately related to a common ancestor. This has been a fundamental tenet of evolution, but findings from the past quarter-century indicate otherwise.

The problem is that the three fundamental categories of life, which all species fall into, do not easily map into a single common ancestor. Instead, as one researcher says, "phylogenetic incongruities can be seen everywhere in the universal tree, from its root to the major branchings within and among the various taxa to the makeup of the primary groupings themselves."[5] What would be needed is a highly complex ancestor that would have been as complex as modern cells yet would have somehow arisen in a short time.

Many evolutionists resolve this problem with the idea of horizontal evolution. That is, perhaps the distribution of genes in the three lineages could have been arrived at if the progenitor was so rudimentary that genetic material was readily exchanged between cells in the same population. The process is roughly akin to what is known as lateral gene transfer in modern cells, but more complicated and on a larger scale. The result would be that evolution would occur between neighbors as much as between parents and offspring. We have no evidence, however, for such a process ever occurring.[6]

Confirmation Testing

One strategy used to accommodate failed predictions is to force-fit the evidence to the theory and its predictions. There is a remarkable unicellular organism (*Euglena gracilis*) that can perform photosynthesis if sunlight is present, but also is mobile and consumes nutrients, such as sugars if they are available. It could be classified as a plant or an animal.

In biology there are many such examples of great variation within the lifetime of an individual. Evolution requires variation, for it is the raw material upon which natural selection operates, but natural selection is supposed to operate on variation between lifetimes, not within a lifetime. The intralifetime variation, such as that observed in *Euglena gracilis*, does not relate to evolution. In fact, the tremendous complexity we find in this humble creature seems to present a problem for evolution, since the theory does not explain how such complexity arose. Nonetheless, evolutionists find *Euglena gracilis* to fit nicely within their theory. As Arthur Lindsey states, "The response of *Euglena* to an environment in which sunlight is present and its life in darkness are an excellent example [of adaptation]. Just how these varied responses may take part in actual evolution is not yet known, but logically they seem an unavoidable result."[7]

It is not surprising that evolutionists interpret the world of biology according to evolution. But in so doing, they often miss the fact that biology sometimes does not fit evolution very well. If the theory is assumed to be true, then there can be no contradictory evidence or false predictions.

When researchers recently discovered that the human brain is genetically unique, the findings were automatically viewed from an evolutionary perspective, in spite of problems the findings raised. The human brain is very much different from that of the other primates. How could so much change take place in so little time? As the lead researcher concluded, human evolution must have been "a privileged process," for it seems that a different type of selective process is needed.[8] In other words, although what we are finding about the development of the human brain contradicts evolution's prediction, the brain must nonetheless have evolved somehow.

These results are awkward for evolution. We have no explanation for how *Euglena gracilis* or the human brain could have evolved. But rather than interpreting such results as falsifying a prediction or otherwise being problematic, they are viewed as discoveries about how evolution must have worked. The evolutionary mechanisms may be unknown, but that does not count against the theory. Negative evidences simply are not allowed.

This brings us to the evolutionary prediction that *the fossil species should form an evolutionary tree.* Ever since Darwin, fossils have been arranged in evolutionary tree patterns, more because evolution is assumed than because of anything we can verify from the fossils themselves. Untold numbers of textbooks and museum exhibits have presented compelling images of fossils arranged in evolutionary tree patterns, complete with connecting lines and arrows. The message is clear and unequivocal: the fossil record reveals an unambiguous evolutionary tree.

What those textbooks and exhibits so often failed to show are the complicating details that make the message less compelling. What the fossil record does clearly reveal are a series of "big bangs" followed by a thinning of the ranks by extinctions. In each "big bang," new species appear, and then they remain unchanged until they reach extinction. Rather than the predicted single trunk leading to many branches and twigs of diversity, what we actually find is close to the opposite: relatively rapid appearance of species followed by a narrowing as species reach extinction.

Gradualism

One of Darwin's predictions was that *evolution occurs gradually* via variations within populations. His friend Thomas H. Huxley was concerned that Darwin had assumed "an unnecessary difficulty in adopting

Natura non facit saltum [nature does not make leaps] so unreservedly."[9] But Darwin's theory would have been much less compelling without it. Imagine if evolution had included the caveat that saltations—rapid leaps—can occur by unknown mechanisms such that new fossil species can appear fully formed. This would have greatly weakened Darwin's premise that species evolve by natural processes. Yes, the fossil record suggested that nature does take jumps, but it was safer for Darwin to question the data than to admit them into his theory:

> The geological record is extremely imperfect and this fact will to a large extent explain why we do not find interminable varieties, connecting together all the extinct and existing forms of life by the finest graduated steps. He who rejects these views on the nature of the geological record, will rightly reject my whole theory.[10]

To satisfy theological naturalism, Darwin would need to steer clear of the supernatural, or anything that could be interpreted as supernatural, and argue for a strictly naturalistic origin of species. He could hardly argue for a naturalistic origin and then propose a theory that suggested a supernatural interpretation.

In its first century, evolution maintained Darwin's hope that the fossil record was incomplete, and most evolutionists carefully avoided the problem of stasis and abruptness in the fossil record. But after a hundred years, with evolution routinely taken as fact, it was safe to question the fossils. Following Huxley, in 1972 Stephen J. Gould and Niles Eldredge proposed their *punctuated equilibrium* hypothesis, which acknowledged the fossil record's pattern of stasis and abruptness. With naturalism firmly in place, evolutionists could now afford to openly speculate about nature's discontinuities.

The result is that punctuated equilibrium embraces the fossil record pattern. Favorable variations are envisioned to spread quickly, as speciation is hypothesized to occur in isolated pockets. This fast-paced process would leave few fossil remains, and the fossils that are preserved come from the large central populations where little or no change takes place. "Thus, the fossil record," Gould concluded 120 years after Darwin, "is a faithful rendering of what evolutionary theory predicts."

But Gould's reasoning is circular. It is not that punctuated equilibrium has been observed and so the nature of the fossil record is explained. Rather, punctuated equilibrium is *assumed* because if evolution is true then we need punctuated equilibrium to explain the fossil record. Gould interprets the evidence according to evolution and then claims the evidence is what evolution predicted.

In fact, evolution can predict a wide range of fossil data. If a sequence of fossils can be arranged, then it is said to be an example of gradualism. Where no such sequence can be found, it is said to be a gap in the fossil record or a possible example of an unknown mechanism of evolution, such as with turtles, which appear fully formed in the fossil record. Evolutionists speculate that the absence of intermediates or transitional forms in the fossil record "could indicate that turtles arose saltationally."[11] In other words, evolutionists do not require gradualistic mechanisms. If species appear abruptly, they can explain this as arising saltationally.

In the words of one late-twentieth-century paleontology text, "The observed fossil pattern is invariably not compatible with a gradualistic evolutionary process."[12] There is a problem either with the fossil record or with the idea that evolution is gradual. To make the data compatible with the theory, "undiscovered fossil forms can be proposed," or "unknown mechanisms of evolution can be proposed." And while neither of these ad hoc hypotheses can be known to be true, they also cannot be known to be false. Though Darwin's claim of gradualism may have sounded like a hard prediction, it was not. Its failure can be accommodated by modifying the theory to include some unknown mechanism.

In addition to rapid change, the fossil record routinely records long periods of stasis—the persistence of a fossil species, unchanged for eons of time. Fossils of Colorado sagebrush vole (a small rodent), for example, dated at almost a million years ago reveal stasis in spite of major climate changes.[13]

Sipunculan worm fossils found in China indicate only limited change dating back to the Early Cambrian. Did these worm species remain essentially unchanged for more than 500 million years?[14] Army ants have "not changed a bit" since the reign of the dinosaurs.[15] Ancient water-lily fossils, though smaller in size, reveal a "precise and dramatic correspondence" with their modern counterparts.[16]

The famous horselike fossil species, often claimed as evidence of gradual change, actually reveal a set of unchanging species, overlapping in time. As with many proposed evolutionary sequences, what the fossil record actually reveals is a scattering of many species that do not fall into an evolutionary lineage.[17] These findings of abrupt change are also reflected at the molecular level, where gene comparisons often reveal a need for rapid appearance followed by stasis.[18]

Just-So Stories

Retroviruses, like other viruses, invade cells and use them to reproduce. What makes retroviruses different is that they insert a copy of their genes into the host cell's DNA. This tiny genetic element is called a provirus, and retroviruses that invade germ cells (i.e., the sperm or egg) pass the provirus on to the offspring. Because the provirus can be passed on to the offspring, it also, according to evolutionists, will be passed on to new descendant species.

Evolution predicts that these *endogenous retroviruses are passed on via common descent.* Their proviruses should appear at the same genetic location within the immense genome of the descendant species. That is, if a common ancestor had a provirus inserted into its genome, then the species derived from it will also have that provirus at the same location within the DNA. Like finding two needles at the same location in two different haystacks, proviruses showing up at the same genetic location in two different species almost certainly would not happen by chance.

This prediction is said to be particularly powerful because it unambiguously reveals common descent relationships. If two species share a common provirus at the same DNA location, then the provirus must have been inherited via common descent—their common ancestor must have had that provirus.

Proviruses have been found that violate this prediction. For instance, one provirus was found in chimpanzees, bonobos, and gorillas, but not humans.[19] But if chimpanzees, bonobos, and gorillas share a common provirus at a common DNA location, then so must humans, according to evolution.

Or again, another provirus is found in several primates but *not* in chimps and gorillas.[20] Because it is found in several primates (including humans), the common ancestor must have had the provirus in its genome. This means that the chimps and gorillas should have the provirus as well. But they do not.

Evolutionists explain these provirus patterns using contingent events in the distant past that we cannot observe. For the provirus that is present in chimpanzees, bonobos, and gorillas but not humans, perhaps it was not completely established in the population of the common ancestor. It had the potential to become established (what geneticists refer to as fixed in the population), or it could die out. And as it was passed along to chimpanzees, bonobos, gorillas, and humans, it became fixed in all but the human lineage.

Regarding the provirus that is absent from chimpanzees and gorillas but present in humans and more distant primates, perhaps a DNA repair process replaced the DNA segment that contained the provirus with a clean version. This same event must have occurred independently in both the chimpanzee and gorilla lineages.

Other explanations are available as well, such as common insertion-site preference. This means that the insertion of a genetic element is not random but tends to occur at preferred locations. These different explanations reveal the malleability of evolutionary theory. Even predictions that are thought to be powerful and unambiguous have a backup when they fail. Fixation, DNA repair, insertion-site preference, and other explanatory mechanisms can account for just about any provirus pattern.

Natural processes operating out of view in the distant past are a rich source of explanatory devices. For instance, another evolutionary prediction is that *molecular differences act like a clock*. This "molecular clock," as the National Academy of Sciences explains, predicts "the time in the past when species started to diverge from one another."[21] But over and over we find the molecular clock to be inaccurate.[22] The many deviations leave the clock's predictive power in question. It does not accurately predict speciation points except when it does, as judged by other evolutionary assumptions. As with the other predictions we have looked at, the molecular clock is more of a problem than a prediction. And the problem is explained with a battery of just-so stories.

Perhaps the clock is perturbed by varying DNA replication accuracies in different species; or perhaps the protein under study has somehow changed its function in its evolutionary history. On the other hand, perhaps a horizontal gene transfer has taken place at some point in the organism's history; or perhaps so many mutations have occurred that the picture has become blurred. Perhaps molecular evolution experiences elevated rates during periods of adaptive radiation, or maybe slightly deleterious mutants were incorporated during population bottlenecks. Perhaps different regions of the genome evolve at different rates for a given species, and perhaps the same region evolves at different rates in different species. Given all these mechanisms, just about any data can be explained.

The Bernoullian Approach

In chapter 4 we saw how statistics have been used to argue for a naturalistic origin of the solar system. Daniel Bernoulli showed that it is highly unlikely that all the known planets in the solar system should fall into roughly the same orbital plane (the ecliptic) if their orbits were randomly determined. Others such as Comte de Buffon and Laplace followed with updated versions of the calculation. All agreed that the solar system design was not random and therefore must have arisen naturally. As Kant explained, the creator would have no reason for placing the planets in a common orbital plane. And if he did, why were they not more precisely aligned?

All of this makes for a curious dichotomy: either the solar system design is random, or it arose strictly via natural processes. Disorder and naturalism were pitted against each other as our only choices. Hence naturalistic theories of the origin of the solar system were not harmed by a wide range of anomalies and exceptions. Laplace was not troubled by Herschel's anomalies—they were interesting research problems. The naturalistic theories may not have worked very well, but they had to be true because the planetary orbits were not random.

Evolutionists use the same type of argument. They say the patterns of design we observe must have arisen via common descent because the patterns are not random. For instance, evolution predicts that *different design features should indicate the same evolutionary tree.* In other words, an evolutionary tree based on one set of data (say the visible features of the species) should be similar to a tree based on a separate set of data (say the molecular features of the same set of species). It would be a daunting task to document the multitude of falsifications of this prediction that have been tallied so far.

The reconciliation of the molecular and the visible, morphological features has been a major problem in trying to resolve the evolutionary tree.[23] The molecular and morphological features often indicate "strikingly different" evolutionary trees that cannot be explained as due to different methods being used.[24]

Mitochondrial protein sequences dramatically conflict with their counterparts from the nucleus and visible features. A late-1990s study found that the mitochondrial DNA provided a statistically high-confidence phylogeny that "was clearly the wrong answer." For example, frogs and chickens were clustered with fish.[25]

The five different types of light-harvesting bacteria do not align. A comprehensive study of their genes showed dramatic inconsistencies.[26] Likewise the growing gap between molecular analyses and the fossil record, concluded one researcher, "is astounding."[27] Instead of a single evolutionary tree emerging from the data, there is a wealth of competing evolutionary trees.[28] And often what evolutionists must conclude is downright strange. Over time insects must have evolved wings, then lost them in the evolutionary process, only to evolve them again later.[29] Or again, bats must have independently evolved, in separate lineages, the same intricate echolocation capability.[30]

Incongruities are found everywhere in the evolutionary tree.[31] The general failure to converge on a single topology has some researchers calling for a break from "tree-thinking."[32]

None of this, however, harms evolution. The design of life, like the design of the solar system, may be difficult for naturalism to explain, but it definitely is not random. The great twentieth-century philosopher Karl Popper had charged that evolution was not falsifiable. Darwinist David Penny responded that evolution would be false if design were random.

Penny computed five different evolutionary trees for the same set of species, generated by five different molecular data sets. As we have seen above, different data sets indicate very different evolutionary trees, causing problems for evolutionary theory. Not surprisingly, Penny's five data sets revealed five different evolutionary trees.

But just as the planetary orbits lie roughly in the same plane, so too biological designs fall into patterns. Penny's five trees, though different, do share similarities. It certainly is a fair conclusion that the biological design patterns are not random, and this was Penny's point. Just as Bernoulli argued that the similar planetary orbits mandated a naturalistic explanation because they were not random, so too Penny argued that similar biological design patterns are a mandate for evolution because they are not random.[33]

It was two and a half centuries later, and the computers and molecular data could not have been imagined by an early-eighteenth-century scientist. But in substance, Penny's calculation was a repeat of Bernoulli's 1734 paper on the solar system. The falsification criterion for naturalistic theories such as evolution is random design. In the face of daunting evidential problems, evolutionists are oblivious to any hint of a theoretical breakdown. All of this arises from the curious dichotomy, mandated by evolutionists, between natural processes and randomness. Disorder and naturalism are pitted against each other as our only choices.

Imagine if objects occasionally floated in midair. Though such observations would defy gravitational theory, they could be labeled statistically insignificant. Obviously this would be a mistake, and this illustrates why science cannot be replaced by statistics. Indeed, often it seems that the exceptions, the anomalies, are what stimulate interesting and important scientific discovery. A theory might work most of the time, but if it breaks down occasionally, this draws the scientist's attention. The rare failure is more interesting than the common success. Rather than use statistics to rationalize unexplained observations, science needs to focus in on such observations.

Predictions in the Genome

Another prediction of evolution is that *similar species have similar genomes*, but the newly sequenced genome data are revealing dramatic differences. Even variants within the same species have large numbers of genes unique to each variant. This was a surprise finding for evolutionists. Initially some evolutionists thought the mystery would resolve when more genomes were analyzed. They predicted that similar copies of these genes would be found in other species. But with each new genome, we find yet more unique genes.

Variants of the *Escherichia coli* bacteria, for instance, each have hundreds of unique genes. And some of these genes have been found to have important functions, such as helping to construct proteins.[34] With evolution we must believe that with every new species or variant there is a rapid influx of new genes, which then often attain important functions.

Further, just as evolution predicts similar genomes in similar species, so also it predicts that *more distant species should have greater differences in their genomes.* In particular, we should not find highly similar DNA sequences in distant species. One evolutionary explanation for such a finding would be that a particular sequence is functionally required. In other words, highly similar DNA sequences in distant species would be maintained by natural selection because only a few such sequences work. But such constraints are not typical.

Histones are a class of proteins that help organize and pack DNA, and the gene that codes for histone IV is highly conserved among different species. Of its hundreds of nucleotides, fewer than half a dozen changes are typically found between different species. Evolutionists had predicted that there must be a strong functional constraint on this protein sequence, allowing for only a few mutations in the gene sequence. But experiments in the laboratory of design theorist Michael Behe showed otherwise. They mutated the histone IV sequence in yeast cells, but the yeast performed just as before.[35]

Even more remarkable are the recently discovered ultra-conserved elements (UCEs), which are completely identical DNA sequences in distant species, such as mouse and human. Could these sequences be so sensitive that even a single mutation could not be allowed? Hardly—in fact, they can be completely knocked out in mice without observable consequence.[36]

We have focused on some of the problems with evolution, but there are positive evidences as well. As with cosmological origins, there is a mix of evidences regarding biological origins. The purely naturalistic story is problematic; this much we can say. But obvious explanations for the origin of species remain elusive. We are left with as many questions as we began with. Theological naturalism has led us down a path of mixed results. The evolution hypothesis sometimes works and sometimes fails. This much is fine. There is nothing wrong when theories do not work very well, for they can still be useful. The flat earth model is routinely used by physicists and engineers.

The problem is that science lacks the perspective to understand its own limitations. There is a tremendous contrast between the state of the evidence and the claim that evolution is a fact. We need to explore naturalistic explanations, but at the same time we need to understand that theological naturalism does not provide a balanced assessment of its own theories.

7

Inherit the Wind All Over Again

It is one of our most captivating and enduring cultural stereotypes: the religious fundamentalist unable to accommodate a changing world versus the objective scientist bringing new truths. Historians call it the warfare thesis, where religion is cast as being at war with science. Evolution skeptics call it "the *Inherit the Wind* stereotype," after the Jerome Lawrence and Robert Lee play and movie. *Inherit the Wind* is a fictionalized account of the famous 1925 Scopes Monkey Trial in Dayton, Tennessee.

Lawrence and Lee wrote *Inherit the Wind* to illustrate the threat to intellectual freedom posed by the anticommunist hysteria of the 1940s McCarthy era. And what better platform to use than religious fundamentalists opposing scientific truths—even if the story is fictionalized? The play was a Broadway hit, and movie and TV versions followed. It is now a classic and is regularly restaged everywhere from the local theater to international venues.

But few people are aware of the story behind the story. This allegory is a fictionalized account, but for many it reveals what they believe to be the core essentials of the origins debate: objective science versus religious dogma. Particular skirmishes may have their own nuances, but isn't this the underlying framework? How important are the details of the summer of 1925 in Dayton? *Inherit the Wind*, so the thinking goes, is an allegory that captures the reality of political and religious dogma opposed to heroic intellectualism.

This is the myth of *Inherit the Wind*. The reality is, as usual, more complicated. While the opposition to evolution in *Inherit the Wind* is portrayed as an intrusion of religion into things scientific, in fact evolution itself is the better symbol of such an intrusion. The story behind the story is that Lawrence and Lee's cultural icon is itself now part of a new kind of anti-intellectualism. The widespread popularity of *Inherit the Wind* and its cultural stereotypes is not a sign of healthy intellectual freedom triumphing over religious intolerance. Rather, it is an unfortunate sign of yet more ignorance and intolerance, as evolutionists are cast as benevolent and objective while skeptics are cast as narrow-minded fundamentalists.

This cultural stereotype is now baked in. News reporters instinctively report on the religion of anyone who would question evolutionary theories, while the naturalists are portrayed as mere scientists. With each new skirmish over the teaching of evolution in public schools in the United States, we are treated to another round of Bible-versus-science headlines. No matter that the skeptics raise scientific concerns: they will be grilled about their religious habits and motives. Evolution, meanwhile, is assumed to be grounded in nothing but empirical observation.

The warfare thesis did not begin with *Inherit the Wind*. A century before, the taunts and antics of Darwin's friend Thomas H. Huxley did much to construct a myth of war between science and theology. Later in the nineteenth century, chemistry professor John W. Draper and Andrew D. White, cofounder of Cornell University, made influential contributions promoting the warfare thesis as a general trend in the relationship between religion and science.

Twentieth-century historians realized these works were more polemical than historical.[1] They are black-and-white renditions of a complicated

history. For instance, how is it that so many scientists are religious? This
hardly supports the warfare thesis. Could it be that, quite the opposite,
religion and science are actually harmoniously allied? After all, modern
science often enjoyed substantial support from the church in the early
years. This is the story told more recently by accommodationists. But like
the warfare thesis, the harmony thesis is a selective view of history.[2]

What so often goes unrecognized is the importance of theological assumptions in the column labeled "Science." As we have seen, theological
naturalism undergirds the historical sciences. With this understanding
we can make clear sense of the warfare and harmony theses. There is
harmony because the idea that God designed and created the world has
been a tremendous motivator in science. The church and science were
often allied in centuries past. But there was conflict too. Theological
naturalism mandated that God did not design the world. Not surprisingly, this would conflict with the traditional view of God as Creator.
Science could be marshaled to support either position. The conflict
was not between science and religion but between different theological
positions. Unfortunately this landscape is rarely understood. In 1692
English theologian Richard Bentley accused Thomas Burnet of atheism.
This charge has often been leveled against openly professing believers. As
we saw in chapter 3, this trend has continued up until today. But from
Burnet to today's Darwinists, a great many naturalists are simply not
atheists. Even those who advanced the warfare thesis, such as Huxley
and White, were often friends with religion. Huxley was sympathetic
to the Church of England, and White spoke well of Christianity.

Far from wishing to injure Christianity, White wrote that he hoped
to promote it—at least, his favored version of Christianity. White's
target was those "mediaeval conceptions of Christianity."[3] Once this
"dogmatic theology" is excised, the separation of God and nature will
be complete, and all will be well:

> My belief is that in the field left to them—their proper field—the clergy
> will more and more, as they cease to struggle against scientific methods

and conclusions, do work even nobler and more beautiful than anything they have heretofore done. And this is saying much. My conviction is that Science, though it has evidently conquered Dogmatic Theology based on biblical texts and ancient modes of thought, will go hand in hand with Religion; and that, although theological control will continue to diminish, Religion, as seen in the recognition of "a Power in the universe, not ourselves, which makes for righteousness," and in the love of God and of our neighbor, will steadily grow stronger and stronger, not only in the American institutions of learning but in the world at large.[4]

White was not promoting naturalism to satisfy some sort of materialism or atheism. Instead, White was promoting what I have been calling theological naturalism. As we saw in chapters 2 through 5, theological premises led to the assumption of naturalism in science. By the late nineteenth century, naturalism was becoming firmly accepted in the sciences. Advocates such as White could then leverage this new truth to chastise those religious elements outside of theological naturalism. Those "medieval conceptions of Christianity" needed to be brought up to date and in line with modern thinking.

White was attempting to achieve harmony by separating science and religion into two different domains. To achieve this, he needed believers to recognize "their proper field"—theological naturalism. A contemporary rendition of this is Stephen Jay Gould's description of NOMA (the nonoverlapping magisteria of science and religion). Not surprisingly, the NOMA approach finds a greater sympathy than Richard Dawkins's hard-edged atheism that attacks any and all religion.

As White put it, theology, once put in its proper place, would be free to do work even nobler and more beautiful than anything done heretofore. We can see how although evolutionary thinking was motivated by theological premises, it is the evolution skeptic who is cast as the religious zealot. No matter how much science he brings to the table, he is viewed as clinging to a medieval conception of Christianity.

A Science Stopper

It is easy to see how naturalism became synonymous with science, and anything else antithetical to science. After all, supernatural causes, such as God creating the world, cannot be analyzed by science. Rather than motivating research, the notion of divine creation was argued to be a science stopper. Darwin complained that with divine creation we can say only that so it is, and this is not a scientific explanation.[5] On the other hand, Darwin argued that the naturalist "has a wide field open to him for further inquiry."[6]

Likewise Darwin's friend J. D. Hooker complained that if theories of divine creation are "admitted as truths, why there is an end of the whole matter, and it is no use hoping ever to get any rational explanation of origin or dispersion of species—so I hate them."[7] And as we saw in chapter 2, Joseph Le Conte declared that to doubt purely natural causation is to "doubt the validity of reason."[8] For his part, Thomas Huxley declared, "I really believe that the alternative is either Darwinism or nothing, for I do not know of any rational conception or theory of the organic universe which has any scientific position at all beside Mr. Darwin's."[9]

The case was now sealed shut. Theological naturalism mandated that the cosmos and life itself must have evolved naturally. And if the data suggested otherwise, well, that did not matter, because nonmechanistic causes were defined to be outside of science anyway. Naturalism was true and then true again. Naturalism was doubly true, for the alternative had to be false and the alternative was unscientific anyway. It was another powerful theological argument for naturalism. Isaac Newton and many other scientists from centuries past had succeeded in science without imposing naturalism. But by the nineteenth century, theological naturalism was dominant. The fact that good science is possible without full-blown naturalism had been forgotten.

Since Darwin, the notion that naturalism is required for science has grown even stronger. Today it is appealed to whenever a challenge arises.

Scientific American recently informed its readers, as though it were a fact, that viewing nature as designed does not expand scientific inquiry but rather shuts it down.[10] Again and again, naturalists explain that those who are not naturalists have no scientific curiosity.

This powerful argument that only naturalism qualifies as genuine science became a principle of our constitutional jurisprudence in the remarkable *Kitzmiller v. Dover Area School District* legal decision. Among other things, U.S. District Judge John E. Jones ruled that "attributing unsolved problems about nature to causes and forces that lie outside the natural world is a 'science stopper.'"[11] After all, Jones reasoned, if an explanation is not based on natural causes, then it simply is not science.[12]

The problem, according to Jones, is that if a scientist attributes a cause to an untestable supernatural force, then "there is no reason to continue seeking natural explanations as we have our answer."[13] Fortunately, as Jones explains,

> since the scientific revolution of the 16th and 17th centuries, science has been limited to the search for natural causes to explain natural phenomena. This revolution entailed the rejection of the appeal to authority, and by extension, revelation, in favor of empirical evidence. Since that time period, science has been a discipline in which testability, rather than any ecclesiastical authority or philosophical coherence, has been the measure of a scientific idea's worth. In deliberately omitting theological or "ultimate" explanations for the existence or characteristics of the natural world, science does not consider issues of "meaning" and "purpose" in the world. While supernatural explanations may be important and have merit, they are not part of science.[14]

This is today's mythology. The seventeenth century's move to naturalism and the science that followed were anything but objective. The idea that they were free of authoritative theological explanations and concerns about meaning and purpose is today's version of history. Today's wisdom is unaware of the theological concerns behind this move. For

Jones there simply are the naturalists whose science is objective and the skeptics with their "deeply held beliefs which drive their scholarly endeavors."[15] Naturalism now has the official legal stamp of approval.

A Closed System

The caricature of evolutionists as merely following the evidence and skeptics as religiously driven has created an environment within science that is intolerant of skepticism. Doubt about naturalism is suppressed since there is little to gain and much to lose by expressing such doubt. Passing grades, letters of recommendation, employment opportunities, and promotions are all at stake. Success will not come easy to those out of line.

A few years ago I applied for a biophysics faculty position at a major research university. I knew that my evolution skepticism might cause concern. But I hoped that my criticism, grounded in scientific and historical analysis, would be intriguing to the faculty search committee. Also, my biophysics research is independent of my skepticism of evolution.

The initial response from the search committee was promising. The chair of the committee, a senior researcher and professor, sent me an encouraging e-mail message. He wrote that the committee was "quite impressed" with my application and that for certain faculty positions I was viewed as "a strong and highly appropriate candidate." We traded further communications dealing with logistics of my application. Two months later, he wrote me a letter with even more good news. It began: "Thank you for permitting us to consider your candidacy for the faculty position in [our department]. The search committee is impressed with your qualifications and research accomplishments. I write to inform you that we have identified you as a candidate for further consideration." The letter went on to provide logistical details of the search process.

This was the final communication I received. Once I was a candidate for serious consideration, my publications were more carefully reviewed, and my skepticism of evolution became clear. Committee members contacted a reference, who assured them that my research was independent of my views on evolution. Nonetheless, skepticism of evolution was unacceptable. My application was rejected, and their search continued. The next year the search committee advertised a similar announcement for faculty positions. I sent another e-mail to the search committee chair, asking if he thought I should apply and if I could transfer my previous application to this new search. The message went unanswered.

For every example like this, there are hundreds more faculty candidates who never bother to apply because they know it is a wasted effort. The difference is that I was more optimistic—or perhaps more naive. This rejection did not hurt my career or leave me bitter, but it was a reminder of how theological naturalism has influenced our institutions. The *Inherit the Wind* stereotype has bred a new form of narrow-mindedness that shuts its ears to any and all criticism of evolutionary theories. Consequently an inbreeding has occurred within academia. On a wide range of disciplines academicians often see both history and contemporary debate through a simplistic and erroneous *Inherit the Wind* filter. In their view there is religious faith and then there is objective research.

Whiggish History

In his 2005 book on the history of the centuries leading up to Darwinism, Oxford's Keith Thomson tries to explain how evolution is nothing more than good science, though history shows it to be a contingent idea, developing out of cultural and religious concerns. How is it that Darwin's idea is a scientific discovery if the general idea had been discussed and urged for centuries before 1859? Thomson must force-fit the historical facts into a Darwinistic narrative that relies heavily on the warfare thesis.

Darwin made many appeals to dysteleology and the problem of evil. Nature's apparent evil and dysteleology seems to counter its complexities.

A century earlier this had been the message from David Hume in his rebuttal to the natural theologians. Thomson's message to the reader is that Hume's point was cogent. Thomson elaborates on Hume's attack and, keeping to a Darwinian view of history, describes it as forceful.[16]

Thomson augments Hume's point with several pages of dysteleology examples, including the oft-cited claim that the vertebrate eye is not designed well. Thomson explains, "No one designing an eye would have put the nerves in front of, and partially blocking, the receptors." It must have evolved, for a designer "would surely have got it right."[17]

But what is "right" when it comes to design? Is judging what is "right" in a design merely a scientific exercise? Thomson seems to believe so. The modern age has brought with it the requirement that God's designs must be materially perfect.[18] This was a consistent doctrine of the natural theologians, such as William Paley, and represents an important element of rationalism in modern theology. It seems self-evident to the rationalist that God would have had only material objectives when designing the world. He certainly would not have intended a materially inefficient design. Today's origins debate inherits these ideas, so understanding this history is important. Thomson spends a good deal of time detailing natural theology but never explores why or how natural theology took this turn. Instead, Thomson simply reinforces this modern assumption.

"Natural theology," explains Thomson, "has a validity only as long as one is able to see the works of nature as perfect."[19] This was how eighteenth-century English natural theology was cast, but it is not, as Thomson claims, a universal requirement of natural theology. The requirement of perfection in nature is historically descriptive, not generally prescriptive. This is crucial, for this rationalistic turn fueled evolutionary thinking. If God would have made nature perfect, according to our sensibilities, and it obviously was not, then God must not have created nature. This was Hume's, and after him Darwin's, powerful argument. Too often commentators today miss the crucial point. Darwin advanced naturalism with religious arguments rather than with compelling scientific explanations.

The Darwinian View of Science

The classic debate between natural theologian and skeptic is steeped in theology and metaphysics. But to hear Thomson tell the story, it was simply another forceful and unmet challenge from the pen of Hume. And if Hume was right, then Paley must have been wrong. Thomson proceeds to give a brittle version of Paley's design argument that easily breaks to pieces.

Paley's famous argument was that just as the complex watch must have a designer, so too biological machines such as the human body must have a designer. Paley extended this argument to include the functions of these biological machines. Not only are organisms highly complex, but they make new copies (reproduction) and obtain their own energy (metabolism). Watches never made new watches, and one must wind the watch for it to operate. As impressive as a watch is, unless wound it lies dormant—a package of intricately designed parts that otherwise does nothing. Biological machines, on the other hand, encompass far greater levels of complexity.

These were cogent points and remain so today. We have learned more details than Paley dreamed of, but his point remains. Paley's design argument was not that the fantastic capabilities of reproduction and metabolism call for God's direct intervention; rather, the argument was that the design was all the more sophisticated, and therefore the design argument all the more obvious. Thomson does not recognize this and casts Paley as advocating a sort of vitalism.[20] Specifically, Paley referred to a "secret spring" within organisms since he was ignorant of the microscopic details. Thomson reads this as a call for "God's own and unique vital power."[21] Rather than acknowledging Paley's point, Thomson forces Paley into a caricature of natural theology that Paley never put forth: "For Paley, whether in the maintenance of life in a single organism, or the generation of one organism from another, or the creation of the very first life, the power of God was needed."[22]

Thomson thus reduces Paley's design argument to an argument for divine intervention rather than divine design. Given this reinterpretation of natural theology, any evidence for naturalistic reproduction or regeneration is fatal to design. And Thomson believes he has found just such evidence:

> If any one fact slayed the hypotheses of the natural theologians, it was the observation of how a simple hydra conducts its vital zoological business. What seems to be one of the lowest forms of life has a great deal to tell us about life itself. Trembley's experiments had been known for fifty years before Paley wrote, but natural theologians had closed their eyes to a whole range of awkward facts such as this.[23]

Yes, the hydra did have "a great deal to tell us about life itself." That simplest of forms was capable of highly complex functions. For instance, when it was cut to pieces each piece grew back to form a new hydra. The hydra, though researchers did not understand how, was capable of automatically regenerating itself. There was no apparent divine intervention required, so should this not have falsified the design argument? Thomson has created a straw-man version of natural theology and now wonders why that damning hydra evidence went unnoticed. The Darwinian historian fails to see that the hydra was simply another complex design requiring a designer. This did not falsify Paley's design arguments; it reinforced them.

Thomson gives an excellent account of how, in the late eighteenth and early nineteenth centuries, population growth and its effects were beginning to be understood. Population growth was geometric, but provisions could increase only arithmetically. Did this not lead to a sort of zero-sum game, where limited resources had to be divided amongst an ever-increasing pool of consumers?

In keeping with his doctrines that creation is perfect and God wills and wishes for our happiness, Paley rationalized population growth. His utilitarian explanations were strained, and they helped to lay the groundwork for Darwin and his concept of the survival of the fittest. Paley was driven by a utilitarian-influenced theology of God and creation. He had to address the issue of population growth, but this was an area where his theology did not apply very well.

It is also yet another example of the contingency of Darwin's theory. Over and over the history of thought reveals the tracks leading to Darwinism. But Thomson never sees the obvious conclusion that the foundation for Darwin's theory was not compelling scientific data but strong theological and cultural concerns.[24] The problems presented by dysteleology, evil, divine intervention, and even population growth were resolved by Darwin's theory. Thomson sees no connection, yet Darwin's theory, though supposedly nothing more than empirically driven science, just happened to scratch where the key metaphysical itches lay.

It seems that at least one reason Thomson fails to see that Darwin's theory is a contingent, rather than objective, finding is that Thomson is sympathetic to those theological and cultural motivators. Thomson's rendition of the history behind the demise of natural theology and rise of evolution is colorful. But at each turn, the message is clear: the reasons behind this move were good. And perhaps the best of these reasons is the evil in the world. Thomson drives home the point in a passage worthy of Darwin himself:

> We adopt the noble lion as a metaphor for strength and bravery, but there is little nobility in being the deer (or child) that is ripped apart by the lion and eaten while its viscera are still quivering in the dust. It is hard to see a divine utilitarian goodness in venomous snakes, stinging wasps, mosquitoes and poisonous plants, or in leprosy, malaria and cancer, or in the miseries of old age and the death of the very young. For humans, ugliness, disharmony, war, tyranny, famine, viciousness, greed, racism, inter-religious and intra-religious conflict seem to be at least as common a part of our conditions as goodness, happiness, peace and beauty.
>
> This is the stalemate debated in every pulpit, denied at the hospital bed, eluded at every graveside—an acid eating away at the faith of young and old. A benign and loving God has somehow to be squared with all the slings and arrows of outrageous fortune that flesh is heir to. If God has not created all this misery and evil, and if they do not flow as some

natural consequence of his creation, we would have to accept that it has some other cause. In that case, God would not be the only First Cause, but one of many possible causes. Given the premises on which it was based, natural theology could not avoid the challenge of finding an explanation of this paradox, to provide a new explanation of why good and evil are equally God's work. This was its Achilles heel, and in the attempt to produce a rational scientific explanation of misery, want and evil, a door was opened for Darwin.[25]

These are powerful theological arguments for naturalism, and yes, they certainly did open a door for Darwin. But his theory had little to do with scientific deduction.

Creationist Brush Fires

Theological naturalism, as exemplified by Thomson, affects the Darwinist's view of today's debate over naturalism as well as the history of science. Just as Thomson tends to view historical figures such as Paley according to the warfare thesis, evolutionists routinely misinterpret today's evolution skeptics. I have seen this repeatedly in the literature and in debate. And recently I had an opportunity personally to witness this version of ignorance.

A school district in my area was being challenged by parents to teach evolution from a neutral perspective. The district was in the process of selecting a new high school biology textbook. As is typical, the text presented a dogmatic version of evolution. All the evidence was portrayed as supporting evolution, and there was no mention of the many evidential problems. The text concluded, "There is overwhelming evidence from fossils and many other sources that living species evolved from organisms that are extinct."[26] It was an erroneous and misleading statement, and the parents challenged the school district to present the evidence more accurately. I was asked to analyze the textbook and point the school district to specific problems. I provided a written review, and I presented slides to the high school science teachers. In the presentation I included brief, simple suggestions for how teachers could present the material to more accurately represent the theory.

What followed was a sort of contemporary reenactment of *Inherit the Wind*, complete with just about every stereotype played out to perfection. The parents' request was brought up at a series of board meetings. In those hot summer nights there was standing room only as the crowd spilled out from the meeting room into the hallway. The parents carefully worked their way through the school district's process for curriculum change, and I helped by presenting the problems with the textbook. But the meetings often became emotional and irrelevant. There were parents who argued against religion in the classroom, as though that was being proposed. A rabbi explained that Genesis must be mythological, and a parent decried a Jehovah's Witness tract. Even the school board members launched into their own diatribes that had little relevance to the case. We were called liars, and at every turn our motives were questioned.

In the end the school district did not feel qualified to judge my review of the textbook, so they asked six evolutionist professors from academia as well as the textbook publisher to evaluate my comments. The professors and publisher were hardly objective critics. But they were in a difficult position, because my review of the text rested on well-accepted biology rather than controversial claims.

The letters from the professors were filled with nonscientific arguments, mischaracterizations of my position, and personal attacks. It was amazing to see such material set forth as a defense of the textbook's inaccuracies. Professor Michael Turelli of the University of California at Davis charged that I was "up to the usual creationist tricks." Professor Arthur Shapiro, also from UC Davis, warned the school board that I was intentionally "throwing powder in the eyes."

Shapiro attempted to reassure the school district that the evidential concerns that I raised "have no bearing on whether evolution occurred."

And how can they be sure of this? Shapiro told the school board members that the nested pattern that species fall into makes evolution a "reality." His point was neither valid nor sound. Not only is this a logical fallacy,[27] but there are so many violations of the nested pattern that the premise is nowhere close to being true. As we saw in chapter 6, evolutionists use this evidence in a Bernoullian sense. As with the planetary orbits, a pattern has been found, and as Bernoulli and Kant argued in the eighteenth century, such patterns must have natural causes. Of course the school board members were unaware that Shapiro's point derived from theological naturalism.

Professor Samantha Hens of California State University at Sacramento attempted to illustrate solid evidence for evolution. She told the school district that the horse sequence is an example of "slow, gradual transformations of one species to another." This was an unfortunate perpetuation of an icon of evolution. The horse sequence has regrettably suffered several faulty interpretations. The idea that it reveals gradual transformations has long since been admitted to be at odds with the evidence. Indeed, Professor Hens's statement is remarkable because often the horse sequence is used as a showcase for why gradualism is *not* generally correct. Ironically, in counseling the school district the professors were exemplifying the sort of argumentation that must be avoided in science.

Hens next tried to reassure the school board of evolution's veracity with a popular sound bite: "Nothing in biology makes sense except in the light of evolution." This is the title of a paper written by Theodosius Dobzhansky (1900–1975), one of the twentieth century's leading Darwinists.[28] Dobzhansky's paper was a tirade against divine creation and is now a classic example of theological naturalism in action. Again, the school board was unaware of the theological doctrine being fed to them.

Professor Nicholas Ewing, chair of the biology department at California State University at Sacramento, warned of ulterior motives: I was surreptitiously attempting to introduce "creation science dogma into a scientific curriculum." Though I criticized the science in the textbook and repeatedly urged that the school district adhere to the state standards, Ewing characterized my material as one of many "brush fires ignited by Creationists," and he urged that "the study of science and religion remain separate and distinct within our education curricula."

Ewing argued that there is no point in teaching problems with evolution for the simple reason that "evolution is fact." He asked the school board members: "Have you ever seen a sea lion try to move across a beach?" It is obviously not a good design, he argued, and so it must have evolved. "That design is not intelligent, but rather is a product of evolution," concluded Ewing, for "design would attempt to produce something that works well, if it is intelligent design, and this does not work well and so is not intelligent design." An empiricist sees evidence for design in the sea lion. The fact that the sea lion moves awkwardly can mean that there is a design tradeoff, or it can mean that this was the intended design. A rationalist, on the other hand, assumes a priori knowledge of intentions. Awkward mobility could not have been intended, so it must have evolved.

Ewing also made a series of erroneous claims about the evidence for evolution. He began with the remarkable statement that "DNA sequences provide an absolute and irrefutable record" that evolution is a fact. "Virtually every single gene sequence we examine," Ewing explained, "can be seen to be represented in closely related species and in more distantly related species with increasing numbers of nucleotide changes as we look at more distant species." It was, Ewing triumphantly concluded, "absolute proof, in hard copy, reiterated in every single gene of every single organism." It sounded good, but it was wrong. Ewing was sounding more and more like the textbook and less like a biology professor. As we saw in chapters 5 and 6, the real data do not fit the evolutionary pattern as Ewing envisioned.

Ewing also attempted to reassure the school board members with another remarkable claim that every piece of evidence in biology supports the conclusion that evolution is a fact. But how could this be? I responded that there are many evidences that do not support this conclusion, such as (1) nonhomologous development pathways, (2) the abrupt appearance of fossil species in the geological strata, and (3) the complexity and circularity of cellular protein synthesis.

To this Ewing responded that these three examples "are not facts." But these are facts—well-known facts. Even the staunch evolutionist Richard Dawkins agrees that such fossils appear "as though they were just planted there, without any evolutionary history." And it would be equally problematic to say that nonhomologous development processes and the complexity and circularity of cellular protein synthesis are not facts. Protein synthesis in the cell is "circular" because it requires pre-existing proteins. A leading undergraduate textbook calls the process "inexplicably complex."[29]

How could a biology instructor explain to his or her students that such well-known and well-documented biological phenomena are not to be considered as facts? Ewing's claim that my examples are not facts, coupled with his insistence that evolution *is* a fact, raised questions about how he was arriving at his conclusions.

One of the points I had made to the school district was the importance of scientific thinking. Students need to understand the difference between facts and theories, for instance. Things that we observe are facts, and to say otherwise goes against the scientific method.

I sent a thirty-page response to the school board, going over each point made by the professors and publisher. My response was detailed and fully referenced, but it was too late. The damage was done. Before I even saw the professor's letters, the school district had acted swiftly and secretly to squash the parents' efforts. And the local newspaper followed in turn with the appropriate rendering of events. The story explained that "the professors who submitted reviews blasted the proposal from Hunter." It was *Inherit the Wind* all over again.

8

Theological Naturalism

Theological naturalists in the centuries leading up to Darwin's time made powerful arguments. Thomas Burnet, the deists, Gottfried Leibniz, Immanuel Kant, and many others pointed to a variety of reasons that the world must have arisen strictly by secondary causes—the laws and processes of nature. This contributed to uniformitarianism and evolutionary thinking in the historical sciences. Today, these ideas predominate in the study of what is appropriately called *natural history*.

Although the driving concern for naturalists was theological and they were not promoting atheism, there can be little doubt that today their ideas have fueled religious skepticism. If there is no divine action, or at least no detectable divine action, then it is understandable that some might take the next logical step to religious skepticism. Kant was defending the faith against atheism in the form of random atomism, but he opened the door to atheism in the form of random naturalism.

But atheism is not the predominant response to Darwin's theory. Darwin's arguments for evolution trace back to the earlier theological naturalists, and not surprisingly he concluded with an appeal to theological naturalism. "To my mind," wrote the primary founder of evolution, "it accords better with what we know of the laws impressed on matter by the Creator, that the production and extinction of the past and present inhabitants of the world should have been due to secondary causes, like those determining the birth and death of the individual."[1]

It was an argument straight out of theological naturalism. A better God creates via laws rather than intervention. Burnet, Leibniz, or Kant could not have put it better. And to prove it Darwin had in hand an approving letter from "a celebrated author and divine" agreeing that evolution led to a noble conception of the deity.[2]

The Reverend Charles Kingsley—who was also a novelist—was highly impressed with Darwin's new theory. He was awed by the facts and, following the theological naturalists, eager to view God as the creator of complete and capable laws rather than having to intervene to fill the voids left by empty laws. Like many others from earlier years, Kingsley argued that this made for a greater god.

Kingsley was one of the first post-Darwin theological naturalists, but his sentiment directly parallels that of the earlier naturalists. The difference is that unlike the earlier naturalists, post-Darwin theological naturalists have the final theory in place. Laplace provided the Nebular Hypothesis, and now Darwin explained the species. Thenceforth the focus would shift from *advocating* naturalism to *explaining* naturalism.

Today's theological naturalists elaborate on how theism fits into the evolutionary framework. Their views are often quite similar to those of the pre-Darwin naturalists, but they have developed the theology in greater detail. The early naturalists argued that divine action ought to be minimized in order to satisfy concerns about dysteleology, evil, salvation, the nature of God, and so forth. Today's theological naturalists, while echoing those views, have moved on to the problem of just how those concerns can be satisfied.

Burnet, Leibniz, Kant, and the rest won the battle, and to the victor goes the spoils. Today's theological naturalists have inherited the problem of explaining just why naturalism works so much better. The problem is not easy. This chapter looks at some of the challenges and how theological naturalists deal with them. It is a fascinating study in contrasts. As we shall see, today's naturalists have a very different perspective on science and its history from those we have seen in the preceding chapters.

A Mandate for Naturalism

As we saw in chapter 2, evolutionary biologist and former Dominican priest Francisco Ayala requires evolution in order to account for biology's design flaws. Ayala claims God would never have created such flaws as wisdom teeth and therefore it would be blasphemy to believe in the creation of the species.

Biology professor Ken Miller argues that God would never want to take credit for such evils as the mosquito.[3] Furthermore, Western religion mandates evolution. "The freedom to act and choose enjoyed by each individual in the Western religious tradition," explains Miller, "requires that God allow the future of His creation to be left open."[4] In other words, evolution must be true and it must be independent of God; otherwise "how could the future truly be open?"[5]

Physicist Howard Van Till argues that a god who created the world and then subsequently set about creating species at different times is "theologically awkward."[6] For this would mean that God withheld capabilities and then later imposed form by coercing his insufficiently equipped creation. Better for God to infuse all the capabilities at the beginning so creation has full functional integrity—it need not be monitored and adjusted by the creator. In chapter 4 we saw such views espoused by Kant. Van Till argues that they also date back to the early church fathers.

Similarly, Ian Barbour dislikes the idea of an interventionist god. Not only is the idea of God's intermittently stepping in "theologically dubious,"[7] but Barbour also warns of ascribing nature's evils to God's divine action. "There seem to be too many blind alleys," writes Barbour, "and extinct species and too much suffering and waste to attribute every event to God's specific action."[8]

Physicist and pastor George Murphy argues that a theology in which God acts directly in the world, without the mediation of created agents, is seriously flawed. Such a view, explains Murphy, misrepresents the biblical picture of God and leads to serious questions about the goodness of creation. In his own view, only very rarely would God act directly in the world. What is needed, according to Murphy, is divine action that is undetectable. The dying Savior on the cross appears to us as the absence of God. Likewise, writes Murphy, "if God's activity in nature is to bear the mark of the cross, it too will be hidden."[9] Murphy points out that denying that God intervenes does not mean denying that God is involved and active in the world.

For physicist and theologian Robert Russell, systematic theology reveals a creator who acts through natural processes described by the laws of nature. What science views as evolution, therefore, is a lawlike process that God controls at the quantum level. What appear to be random mutations are the result of "non-interventionist divine action." By this Russell means that God's directing of the evolutionary process is undetectable.[10]

On the other hand, Anglican John Polkinghorne sees divine action as a "top-down" mechanism. God doesn't control the world via subatomic particles all working together to effect macro events. Rather, God controls events in a way analogous to the way humans perceive their willed actions. From my perspective, I simply move my arm. I do not initiate nerve impulses in order to activate muscle contractions leading to appendage movement. Like Russell, Polkinghorne requires that divine action, however it is achieved, is undetectable: "By bringing the world into existence God has self-limited divine power by allowing the other truly to be itself. The gift of Love must be the gift of freedom, the gift of a degree of letting-be."[11]

And does this not help solve the problem of evil? Just as God's gift of free will carries with it the downside of moral evil, Polkinghorne argues that God's gift of a free and open creation (a creation with an undetermined future) carries with it the potential for natural evil. Biological evolution, for example, can produce new life forms, but it can also produce deadly viruses. This is "the necessary cost of a creation given by its Creator the freedom to be itself."[12] Polkinghorne concedes that evolution does not seem sufficient to explain the species. For this he considers the need for a higher level of holistic laws of nature. The theological need for undetectable divine action overrides scientific problems that may arise.

Systematic theologian John Haught gives several theological reasons for strict naturalism in the historical sciences, including the god of the gaps and intellectual necessity arguments. "To introduce ideas about God as the 'cause' of natural phenomena at soft points in our scientific inquiries," explains Haught, "is intellectually inappropriate and theologically disastrous."[13]

These views are typical of today's theological naturalists. Their theological views are varied, but the common thread is methodological naturalism. Divine action must not be detectable. It is hardly surprising, therefore, that theological naturalists accept evolution as a scientific fact.

Evolution as Fact

In 1859 Charles Darwin presented his theory of evolution to the world. Of course he could not explain how biology's complexities—designs that remain a challenge to understand even today—arose on their own. Darwin's long book meandered through a variety of evidences, and he supplied thought experiments arguing for evolution. The arguments were circumstantial and subjective and often could just as easily be reversed. The real power behind Darwin's theory was the problems that the biological evidences posed for divine creation. Darwin repeatedly argued that while he could make sense of the data with his new theory, notions of divine creation utterly failed.[14]

Theological naturalism had laid a foundation for Darwin. Naturalistic processes occurring via secondary causes was already the mechanism of choice in cosmology and the fledgling theories of the origin of the species. Darwin's theory was something of a capstone for this movement. And the proof of his theory was the failure of divine creation. As Stephen Jay Gould puts it:

> Odd arrangements and funny solutions are the proof of evolution—paths that a sensible God would never tread but that a natural process, constrained by history, follows perforce. No one understood this better than Darwin. Ernst Mayr has shown how Darwin, in defending evolution, consistently turned to organic parts and geographic distributions that make the least sense.[15]

The designs of species tend to cluster, so that within a genera several clusters of species may be found. Species within a cluster, Darwin observed, "apparently have restricted ranges." The same can be said of the different varieties with a species. Darwin concluded that patterns such as these were "utterly inexplicable if species are independent creations."[16]

Just as Kant claimed that God would not have created the planets in a plane (the ecliptic), so too Darwin argued that God would not have designed species according to the observed pattern. Many of Darwin's arguments involved patterns of design. For instance, there were many similar crustaceans, fish, and other marine animals inhabiting the seas off the eastern and western shores of North America, the Mediterranean and Japan, and the temperate lands of North America and Europe. This, Darwin argued, was "inexplicable on the theory of creation."[17] We cannot rationalize such similarities as due to the nearly similar physical conditions of the areas, for elsewhere similar physical conditions (such as South America, South Africa, and Australia) could be found with utterly dissimilar inhabitants.[18] Likewise, deep limestone caverns on different continents presented nearly identical conditions yet harbored dissimilar species.[19]

Another problem for the doctrine of creation was that native plants and animals are often overtaken by those introduced by human beings. Darwin pointed out that many of "the best adapted plants and animals were not created for oceanic islands; for man has unintentionally stocked them far more fully and perfectly than did nature."[20] If God had created the species, they would have been optimally designed for their specific environments.

Similarly, frogs, toads, and newts were found on only certain islands, such as New Zealand, New Caledonia, and the Andaman Islands. Darwin argued these were not genuine oceanic islands. Aside from these islands, the lack of frogs, toads, and newts was "very difficult to explain" on the theory of creation.[21]

Furthermore, unique species of bat were found on various islands. Why, asked Darwin, "has the supposed creative force produced bats and no other mammals on remote islands?"[22] Islands off South America harbored species similar to those on the South American continent, and likewise islands off Africa harbored species similar to African forms, even though the islands were probably more similar to each other than to their respective mainlands. "Facts, such as these," explained Darwin, "admit of no sort of explanation on the ordinary view of independent creation."[23]

Darwin argued that organs that appeared to be highly developed are probably of high importance, yet they vary greatly between species. "Why should this be so?" he asked. "On the view that each species has been independently created, with all its parts as we now see them, I can see no explanation."[24]

Or again, Darwin asked, "why should that part of the structure, which differs from the same part in other independently created species of the same genus, be more variable than those parts which are closely alike in the several species? I do not see that any explanation can be given."[25]

Darwin also argued that while the webbed feet of ducks and geese are obviously formed for swimming, there are geese that rarely go near the water. And conversely, there are aquatic birds whose toes are bordered only by membrane. Darwin argued these designs did not always fit the environment.

And yet again, there were other aquatic birds with long toes and no membrane, a design good for walking over swamps and floating plants. Darwin argued that aquatic birds should have webbed feet and upland birds should not have webbed feet. Instead, there was a dizzying array of variations suggesting that habits have changed without a corresponding change of structure. Did this not all reveal the failure of creation?[26]

Moreover, biology rarely revealed unique organs designed for some special purpose. Darwin noted that the supposedly independently created species shared many similar organs. "Why, on the theory of Creation, should there be so much variety and so little real novelty?"[27] Just as Kant had argued that divine creation would result in no celestial patterns, so too Darwin argued that divinely created species should not fall into patterns. For Kant, if God created the solar system, then the planets should circle the sun in unrelated, random orbits. And for Darwin, if God created the species, then should we not find "a sudden leap from structure to structure?"[28] As Darwin pointed out, "We never find the bones of the arm and forearm, or of the thigh and leg, transposed."[29]

When equine species are crossed with species from distant parts of the world, the stripes of the offspring resemble not those of the parents but those of other species of the genus. Echoing Leibniz, Darwin argued that the view that such species are independent creations "makes the works of God a mere mockery and deception."[30] The evidence was not merely suggesting problems with the theory of special creation; it was mandating that special creation be false.

Furthermore, similar organs and structures could hardly be optimal designs. Paley and the natural theologians called for a perfect world, but how could similar designs in different species be perfect? "We cannot believe," Darwin pointed out, "that the similar bones in the arm of the monkey, in the fore leg of the horse, in the wing of the bat, and in the flipper of the seal, are of special use to these animals."[31] Then there was the astonishing waste of pollen by fir trees and those many organs bearing "the plain stamp of inutility,"[32] which were utterly inexplicable by special creation. And certainly "no one supposes that the stripes on the whelp of a lion, or the spots on the young blackbird, are of any use to these animals."[33] With divine creation falsified, Darwin concluded, "we may safely attribute these structures to inheritance."[34]

But what about nature's many complexities? David Hume had criticized the design argument for anthropomorphizing God by comparing God's works to human works. Similarly, Darwin pointed out that while it is tempting to see God as the master engineer who crafted complex organs such as the eye, this would make God too much like human beings. Darwin agreed that the perfection of the eye reminds us of the telescope, which resulted from the highest of human intellect. Was it not right to conclude that the eye was also the product of a great intellect? This may seem the obvious answer, but Darwin warned against it, for we should not "assume that the Creator works by intellectual powers like those of man."[35] Better to imagine the eye as the result of natural selection's perfecting powers rather than having God too much involved in the world.

These are some of Darwin's powerful arguments for his theory, and these types of arguments remain today as the powerful evidences for evolution.[36] New theories are often inspired by the failures of older theories. Evolutionary thinking was a response to problems with divine creation. The difference here is that the older theory was mainly theological. It was not a case of compelling positive evidence coupled with the downfall of a religious belief. Darwin and his followers had little idea how complexities could actually arise on their own—the powerful arguments were that divine creation had failed.

The *Bridgewater Treatises* were written by eight eminent scientists, according to the will of the earl of Bridgewater, who died in 1829, for the purpose of demonstrating "the Power, Wisdom, and Goodness of God, as manifested in the Creation."[37] But how could the goodness of God be demonstrated by nature's predation and parasites?

William Buckland (1784–1856) was one of the authors. He interpreted nature's death and bloodshed, which after all was relatively swift and painless, as a divine "dispensation of benevolence."[38] He argued that modern science revealed the "infinite wisdom and power and goodness of the Creator."[39] William Kirby (1759–1850) pointed out the amazing complexities of parasites. How did the parasitic wasp know how to avoid injuring the vital organs?

> The larva of the [parasitic wasp], though every day, perhaps for months, it gnaws the inside of the caterpillar, and though at last it has devoured almost every part of it except the skin and intestines, carefully all this time it avoids injuring the vital organs, as if aware that its own existence depends on that of the insect upon which it preys![40]

Such explanations were hardly soothing for theological naturalists. Centuries earlier Thomas Burnet, Ralph Cudworth, John Ray, and others had called for a distancing of God at the sight of far less wrenching evils. Imagine what their response would have been to the new round of atrocities in nature being uncovered by science. It probably would have been similar to Darwin's response, who found the queen bee's instinctive hatred for her own fertile daughters and the parasitic wasp feeding within the living bodies of caterpillars as yet more proofs for evolution.[41] It seemed that Darwin was, as one historian put it, "yearning after a better God than God."[42] As he wrote to Asa Gray in 1860:

> I own that I cannot see as plainly as others do, and as I should wish to do, evidence of design and beneficence on all sides of us. There seems to me too much misery in the world. I cannot persuade myself that a beneficent and omnipotent God would have designedly created the [parasitic wasp] with the express intention of their feeding within the living bodies of caterpillars, or the cat should play with mice.[43]

Science and religion were "thoroughly interwoven in Darwin's life and thought,"[44] and it is not surprising that theologians gave a warm welcome to Darwin's theory. Nor is it surprising that Darwin's theory would lend itself to a new round of theological naturalism. Theological naturalism had argued for a distancing of the creator from creation. Now Darwin's theory was filling in the details. It was natural selection, not a divine finger, that did the job. Darwin's idea provided a new framework for continued theological speculation.

Science without a Blind Spot

Although the historical contingency of Darwin's theory is obvious, it is often ignored. The parallels between today's theological naturalists and those of the seventeenth and eighteenth centuries are striking, yet they typically go unnoticed and unexplored. Instead, Darwin's theory of evolution is seen as a watershed event—a brilliant and illuminating new finding that overcame outdated beliefs. Earlier evolutionary ideas are seen as fledgling steps toward the truth motivated not by theological concerns but by glimpses of the scientific evidence. And the powerful theological arguments for naturalism are typically ignored.

Of course this is understandable. An idea that is motivated by particular theological concerns is viewed as less compelling than one motivated by empirical evidence. And contingent ideas are viewed as less compelling than fresh, unexpected findings. It is the difference between a cultural trend and a scientific theory.

According to John Haught, evolution does not incorporate theological considerations. Haught agrees that in recent decades religious skeptics have interpreted evolution in terms of atheism, but aside from this extreme view, he says, evolutionary biology has traditionally "stayed away from religion."[45] Likewise, Ted Peters, professor of systematic theology, and Martinez Hewlett, professor of molecular biology, write that while evolution may have fueled skeptical ideologies, evolutionary biology itself is solid science, and it provides new knowledge about the natural world.[46] Polkinghorne and Russell also see evolution as a neutral scientific finding, and Murphy sees Darwin as providing an empirically based finding for theology to consider.

This is the overriding view of today's theological naturalists. Not only does theology mandate naturalism, but science has independently corroborated this result. This theological consilience with evolution is, they say, strictly after the fact. There is no theological motivation for evolution—it is "just science."

Such a convergence of findings is a powerful prescription for naturalism. And if naturalism is true, then there certainly is no blind spot in the historical sciences as I have described in earlier chapters. The historical sciences assume naturalism, and for theological naturalists that assumption poses no risk; rather, it is the appropriate assumption.

Furthermore, if naturalism is true, then why make a distinction between the historical and experimental sciences? The historical sciences may have less data to work with, but otherwise the problem is the same. Our knowledge of natural laws is used to model the data and understand what occurred, whether five minutes ago in the laboratory or five billion years ago in the cosmos.

The Dilemma

Theological naturalists see a consilience between religion and science. Science just happens to corroborate our concepts of God and creation, and so theological naturalism has prospered. This does not mean, however, that all the questions have been answered. In fact many difficult problems remain, such as, for example, where to place our faith in God.

Kant described a God who does not directly create but instead sets up laws that do the creating, while the historical sciences have filled in the details. For Kant, one proof of God was our innate moral sense. This was the spiritual domain. But can this claim withstand the tide of naturalism? As Haught puts it, the historical sciences now "claim to have demystified the outer world unveiling the apparent 'pointlessness' of an essentially lifeless and mindless universe."[47] The momentum of naturalism has today led to claims that even Kant's innate moral sense is nothing but a product of unguided, mindless evolutionary processes.

What then is theological naturalism's solution? First, Haught points out that although science can describe, measure, and even predict, it can never answer the ultimate why questions. Why, Haught asks, does nature have a narrative character at all? Does this not invite theological comment? Though biologist Ursula Goodenough is not a theist and sees the universe as pointless, she nonetheless finds it to have a "sacred depth." Perhaps this sentiment can provide theological naturalism with a path toward maintaining a place for faith. Murphy points to a type of existentialism as a solution to this problem.[48]

Another problem is that undetectable divine action is hardly the story told in the Bible. It is true that Jesus softened hearts and opened minds, but the scriptures are also filled with divine action that the onlookers had no problem describing as miracles. Kant's idea that God ought to work only via lawlike processes is a reinterpretation of scripture, and one can hardly blame religious skeptics for taking the next step. It is understandable that atheists are not moved by the fact that science may not be able to answer the ultimate why questions or that some find a "sacred depth" to the cosmos.

These challenges for theological naturalism are a consequence of its commitment to the position that divine action must be undetectable. It might seem ironic that the church advocates naturalism in the historical sciences. After all, is this not a battle between religion and science? But we have seen that the warfare thesis has its flaws. Burnet, Leibniz, Kant, and the others were theists, so it should not be surprising that many in the church today also advocate naturalism.

9

Moderate Empiricism

Rationalism begins with universal criteria—premises or axioms about the form of the result. And once the result is obtained, it is more likely to be viewed as universal—not merely a useful model but a truth about the world. Rationalism appeals to the desire to work within a framework or unifying principle. As one philosopher wrote:

> The typical rationalist will believe that theories that meet the demands of the universal criterion are true or approximately true or probably true. . . . The distinction between science and non-science is straight-forward for the rationalist. Only those theories that are such that they can be clearly assessed in terms of the universal criterion and which survive the test are scientific. . . . The typical rationalist will take it as self-evident that a high value is to be placed on knowledge developed in accordance with the universal criterion. This will be especially so if the process is understood as leading towards truth. Truth, rationality, and hence science, are seen as intrinsically good.[1]

This well describes theological naturalists. Their universal criteria are the various theological reasons that mandate naturalistic explanations.

131

These naturalistic accounts are taken to be true, though the details may not be completely understood. It is beyond question that true science is defined by their naturalistic approach, and other approaches are not only nonscientific but nefarious. For these rationalists, naturalism is true, the way of science, and intrinsically good. Today, skeptics of evolution are often described as attacking science.

As we saw in chapter 8, Darwin's proofs of evolution were nature's odd arrangements and funny solutions, paths that a sensible God would never tread, as Stephen J. Gould puts it. Darwin presented an inventory of awkward empirical evidence that hardly forced one to conclude for his theory. Darwin could provide only speculations as to how this or that biological design may have arisen naturally, yet he was altogether bold in his pronouncements of the ultimate truth of this theory. For Darwin some form of evolution had to be true because it was theologically mandated. And he equated naturalistic approaches with science. The particulars of the naturalistic hypothesis were less important. One could believe in the views of Lamarck, Geoffroy St. Hilaire, Chambers, or Alfred Russel Wallace instead of Darwin's theory. What was important was to believe in a naturalistic account—this was what allowed for science inquiry.[2]

And as Kingsley had written to Darwin, this led to a noble conception of the deity. Did not naturalism led to a greater God? As Andrew Dickson White explained, with evolution, "science has given us conceptions far more noble, and opened the way to an argument from design infinitely more beautiful than any other developed by theology."[3]

After Darwin, this sentiment that naturalism defines science, is true, and is intrinsically good grew ever stronger. Joseph Le Conte explained that evolution is a law, not a theory, and it is a law to which every department of natural studies must adhere. It is not merely as certain as gravity, "Nay, it is far more certain."[4] Similarly, Teilhard de Chardin maintained that "evolution is a light which illuminates all facts, a trajectory which all lines of thought must follow—this is what evolution is."[5]

In 1951 George G. Simpson wrote that there really is no point nowa-
days in continuing to collect and to study fossils simply to determine
whether evolution is a fact. The question, concluded Simpson, has been
decisively answered in the affirmative. Scientist and social critic Ashley
Montagu elevated evolution beyond all other theories. It was, according to Montagu, "the most thoroughly authenticated fact in the whole
history of science."[6] And Harvard's Ernst Mayr recently explained that
the fact of evolution is so overwhelmingly established that it would be
irrational to call it a theory.[7]

This opinion is now widely proclaimed, and it reveals a metaphysical
certainty. As in the nineteenth century, evolution is convincing today
not because of the science but because of the theology. Evolutionists
such as Mark Ridley present empirical evidences from biology that, if
anything, leave us with more questions than answers. But in his textbook
Ridley asserts that the naturalistic account must be true. His strong
arguments are from theological naturalism. Following Bernoulli, Ridley cites the patterns in biological designs, such as the DNA code and
genetic similarities, that he *knows* would not be manifest if the species
had independent origins. Like the planets, they must have a unified
natural cause. And he explains that poor designs and design similarities
prove that the species must not have independent origins. According to
Ridley, we need a naturalistic account, and furthermore this approach
is the only one that is scientific. If we were to posit a designer, then this
would leave us with an infinite regress problem: who designed the designer? "In the scientific version of the theory which we are concerned
with here," Ridley states, "supernatural events do not take place."[8] As
the philosopher explained above, the distinction between science and
nonscience is straightforward for the rationalist.

Like Ridley, Professor Emeritus George C. Williams has a long list
of reasons that naturalistic accounts must be true. The sun's purpose,
explains Williams, is to illuminate the earth. Why then would it be so
far away, and why would it be enormously larger than the earth? This
makes for a wasteful design, for the earth's small size and great distance

from the sun mean that the earth intercepts only a tiny fraction of the sun's light. What should we expect of a system that is designed to illuminate the earth? Something more efficient, to be sure. Williams suggests a precisely shaped and brightly polished reflector mounted behind the sun to reflect wasted light toward the earth. As it is, the real earth-sun system "shows no such evidence of purposive engineering."[9]

Biology, according to Williams, also reveals gross deficiencies that reveal no intelligent planning. We have only two eyes, yet six muscles to control each eye. We certainly could use more eyes, and we don't need so many controlling muscles. For Williams, "the paucity of eyes and excess of their muscles seem to have no functional explanation."[10] Indeed, it seems that we are plagued with dysfunctional design features from head to toe, and there is "no evidence that God has any engineering expertise." But the problem is not merely inefficiency. A forest may be beautiful, but any tree will almost certainly be afflicted with pests and diseases. Any monkey will show the ravages of fleas or ticks or fungi. Monkeys live in constant danger from attacks. Nature, says Williams, is a tale of relentless arms races, misery, and slaughter.[11]

Similarly, Distinguished Professor Douglas Futuyma declares that nature is full of useless features, inadequate design, shoddy workmanship, and harshness or cruelty. Comparing the anatomies of various plants or animals, notes Futuyma, we find similarities and differences where we should least expect a creator to have supplied them. Is it not strange that a creator should have endowed bats, birds, and pterodactyls with wings made out of the same bony elements that moles use for digging and penguins use for swimming?[12]

Birds and mammals are warm-blooded, and for blood transport from the heart they have only one aortic arch, instead of two as in amphibians and reptiles. But birds retain the right aortic arch, while mammals retain the left one. Why the difference? Bacteria have "silent" genes that are never expressed and appear to have no function. The panda's "thumb" is a clumsy design, and no caterpillars have compound eyes. Photosynthesis is immensely useful, yet no higher animals have this mechanism.

Futuyma argues strenuously that these and many other examples of shoddy design prove the species arose from natural causes. From our wisdom teeth to our need for vitamin C, biology reveals a lack of design. Take any major group of animals, Futuyma remarks, and the poverty of imagination that must be ascribed to a creator becomes evident. Why should there be more than a million species of animals and more than half a million of plants? And "what could have possessed the Creator," asks Futuyma, "to bestow two horns on the African rhinoceroses and only one on the Indian species?"[13]

Even worse than all this are the many evils in nature. Male elephant seals battle furiously for females, and many die of bloody wounds. The peacock has such long feathers that it can hardly fly. Sickle-cell anemia afflicts those who have inherited a disastrous gene. Species overproduce, causing overpopulation. Lungworms infest snakes, and schistosome worms kill hundreds of thousands of people each year. And more than 90 percent of the species in history became extinct. It is abundantly obvious to Futuyma that this world was not designed by anything but natural causes. How could a wise creator allow such evils?[14]

Professor Kenneth Miller agrees that in many ways biology reveals that the species were not designed. For example, if silent genes were designed, then the designer made serious errors. And what about the dozens of elephantlike fossils? "This designer has been busy! and what a stickler for repetitive work!" In fact, tallying up all the millions of different species ever found, the creator must have been constantly at work, and this too, for Miller, is hard to believe.[15] For Miller, it could not be more obvious that the species evolved, because they must not have been designed. Likewise, science writer Martin Gardner says that "because there are millions of insect species alone, this requires God to perform many millions of miracles. I cannot believe that."[16]

Stephen Jay Gould contends that orchids seem to be made of spare parts. "If God had designed a beautiful machine to reflect his wisdom and power," writes Gould, as though informing his readers of another scientific fact, "surely he would not have used a collection of parts generally fashioned for other purposes. Orchids were not made by an ideal engineer; they are jury-rigged from a limited set of available components. Thus, they must have evolved from ordinary flowers."[17]

According to Steve Jones, the eye structure could be improved by "the feeblest of designer." This and other examples, says Jones, shows that complex organs are "not the work of some great composer but of an insensible drudge: an instrument, like all others, built by a tinkerer [i.e., the evolutionary process] rather than by a trained engineer."[18] For Michael Ruse, the facts of biogeography mandate an account that does not include a designer. "Given an all-wise God," writes Ruse, "just why is it that different forms appear in similar climates, whereas the same forms appear in different climates? It is all pointless without evolution."[19]

Edward Dodson and Peter Dodson argue that if God had created the species, then they should be distributed uniformly about the globe. "Had all species been created in the places where they now exist, then Amphibian and terrestrial mammals should be as frequent on oceanic islands as on comparable continental areas. Certainly, terrestrial mammals should have been created on these islands as frequently as were bats."[20] For Niles Eldredge, the pattern of design among the species rules out design. "Could the single artisan," he asks rhetorically, "who has no one but himself from whom to steal designs, possibly be the explanation for why the Creator fashioned life in a hierarchical fashion—why, for example, reptiles, amphibians, mammals, and birds all share the same limb structure?"[21]

Evidential problems and quandaries become less important when naturalism is a fact. It is easy to see why the many problems we saw in chapters 5 and 6 do evolution no harm. The theory is assumed to be a fact, so problems are interpreted as unanswered questions—details that are still being worked out. And there is nothing to be gained by questioning a rationalist's universal criteria. For an evolutionist, it is obvious that God would not create all those species. If you question the empirical evidence, then you will be asked to supply a better theory—and it must pass rationalism's universal criteria.

An Alternative to Rationalism

The empirical approach is much less certain about the form of the result. And at the end of the investigation, it is less certain about the truthfulness of the result. Problems are complicated, and humanity is not always up to solving them completely. The empirical approach is not as tidy as the rational approach. But it also does not constrain itself to preconceived notions. It is more amenable to new and unexpected results. All of this came to the fore in the seventeenth century, when the Aristotelians and Cartesians promoted their respective rational approaches as ways of doing science and the members of the Royal Society advanced what one historian referred to as "moderate empiricism."[22]

As we saw in chapter 2, the Aristotelians described phenomena in terms of qualities and forms. Scientific observations were fitted into this framework. And while the Cartesians rejected Aristotelianism, their replacement ideas were equally rationalistic. It appeared to the moderate empiricists that both the Aristotelians and the Cartesians had smuggled in unwarranted a priori assumptions into their investigations. They were both, it seemed, more constrained by their prejudices than guided by reason.[23]

Francis Bacon had criticized Aristotelians for making an unwarranted leap from limited and superficial observations to sweeping generalizations. Likewise the moderate empiricists criticized both the Aristotelians and the Cartesians for declaring their speculations as truths. It all made sense to the rationalists, because their new truths flowed from their axioms. But these axioms were not self-evident. For those who did not see why they should be held as true, the program seemed pointless.

How could the rationalists be so sure of their axioms? They seemed to lack any sense of uncertainty, though they were dealing with lofty hypotheses and insufficient data. There was, it seemed, an overconfidence in the powers of the human intellect. In response, empiricists such as Robert Boyle (1627–1691) spoke of "our dim and narrow knowledge," and Joseph Glanvill (1636–1680) wrote that "ignorance and error" are inescapable in our mortal state.[24]

It is good not to be overconfident, but would not such pessimism regarding our cognitive abilities lead to outright skepticism? Indeed, the moderate empiricists sometimes referred to themselves as such, and Boyle's book title *The Sceptical Chemist* would seem to confirm this warning. But theirs was not a true skepticism. They were skeptical when compared to the rationalists, but in fact the moderate empiricists were quite willing to consider science as able to provide new truths. Boyle could simultaneously extol the human intellect and our ability to learn from science and yet urge extreme caution:

> If men were to set themselves diligently and industriously to make experiments and collect observations, without being over-forward to establish principles and axioms, believing it uneasy to erect such theories . . . not that I at all disallow the use of reasoning upon experiment, or the endeavoring to discern as early as we can the confederations, and differences, and tendencies of things . . . men [should] forbear to establish any theory, till they have consulted with . . . a considerable number of experiments, in proportion to the comprehensiveness of the theory to be erected on them.[25]

A comprehensive or lofty theory, Boyle noted, needs a considerable number of experiments. Likewise Isaac Newton could on the one hand issue his famous retort to the rationalists—"Hypotheses non fingo"[26] (I frame no hypotheses)—declaring that he would not speculate on the ultimate nature of gravity, and yet on the other hand issue his own set of hypotheses on matters less metaphysical.

A hypothesis on the nature of gravity requires metaphysical premises or reasoning. Newton was content to describe the action of gravity and stop there, rather than to speculate further about the ultimate nature of gravity. Today we use the term *underdetermined* to describe theories that go beyond the data at hand.

This ability to maintain a balance between rationalism and skepticism, too much certainty and too much doubt, latching on too tightly and giving up altogether, distinguished the moderate empiricists and gave them a distinctive and powerful investigative approach. Where the rationalist has narrowed the choices, thus cutting off scientific research areas, and the skeptic has given up, thus removing the motivation for research, the moderate empiricist forges new ground, not completely sure but confident that nature's secrets are not completely unattainable either.

It was a stark contrast to Descartes, for whom certainty was crucial. The possibility of being wrong had deeply influenced Descartes and shaped his approach. Doubt everything, Descartes urged, that cannot be absolutely known to be true. Geometrical proofs could provide certainty in mathematics. Descartes sought a high level of certainty in all areas, not just mathematics.

Needless to say, probabilistic thinking was of little interest to Descartes. The moderate empiricists, on the other hand, encouraged scientists to weigh the likelihood of different possible explanations. It would be absurd to reject hypotheses merely because they could not be known to be true, for such proof simply was not possible for many fields of investigation. It would be, as John Wilkins, the first president of the Royal Society, put it, "irrational" to doubt or deny simply because absolute proof is not available.[27]

And so the moderate empiricists were leery of a priori assumptions. Of course this included a priori metaphysical assumptions that declared truths about reality. But it also included a priori methodological assumptions, such as Cartesian doubt and its requirement for absolute proof. Rather than devise an elaborate philosophy of science, the moderate empiricists viewed science as an exercise in common sense. They eschewed an explicitly defined methodology for future investigations of phenomena that were not yet understood. If a genuine gain in new knowledge is sought, then we must admit we do not know what we may discover. And if we do not know what we may discover, how can we dictate how it should be discovered by science? It makes no sense to constrain the methodology of an investigation into the unknown. As

Burns put it, the moderate empiricists contended that the way to become a scientist is to practice actually being one rather than to indulge in a priori theorizing about method.[28] And that practice might be informed by any number of different sources of knowledge.[29]

What Goes Around Comes Around

Perhaps it should not be surprising that this seventeenth-century history from the early days of science closely parallels today's debate. Today's rationalists make arguments strikingly similar to those of the seventeenth-century rationalists. Evolutionists, for instance, embrace their own metaphysical and methodological a priori assumptions. Evolution must be true, and any positing of the supernatural is outside of science. Only naturalistic processes are allowed within the gates of scientific research. Today this is referred to as *methodological naturalism.*

But the concerns of theological naturalism are valid, and we need to consider them carefully. The urge toward naturalism is understandable, and charges of atheism and materialism are unfounded and unhelpful. But the rationalists also need to be careful. With their metaphysical and methodological a priori axioms in place, rationalists make high truth claims. Their powerful epistemological foundation allows them to firmly pronounce what is true and what is false. How often do we hear that this or that evidence *proves* evolution to be true? A little bit of data goes a long way when one has the framework of theological naturalism already in place. The universally held position is that evolution is not a model or hypothesis but an undeniable fact. In all this there is an unspoken dependency on controversial premises.

Today's empiricists, on the other hand, have a much less coherent story to tell. They doubt the purely naturalistic explanation, but like the moderate empiricists of the seventeenth century, they lack the sort of well-defined philosophical assumptions that rationalists enjoy. The evidence for design seems abundantly clear, but what does it mean? For instance, does it make evolution false? Not necessarily. For empiricists, the scientific information we have does not readily convert to comprehensive explanations that we can know to be true. When it comes to origins, we are still left with many questions. Of course empiricists have their own opinions about these questions, but they differ among themselves, and typically they are less sure than are rationalists.

One reason that empiricists lack well-defined philosophical assumptions is the complexity of these issues. For instance, where rationalists are quick to employ the infinite regress to argue for naturalism, empiricists engage in lengthy, detailed debates about what it portends. Likewise for the problem of evil, dysteleology, greater god argument, and so forth. In empiricism, axioms are carefully weighed for all possible implications. For empiricists, the theological and philosophical issues are not to be ignored, yet they are also not to be given superficial treatment. Empiricists differ among themselves and feel free to proceed with the science without having all the difficult questions firmly resolved.[30]

What does seem clear to empiricists is that the answers mandated by rationalists to these difficult questions are debatable. It is not that the rationalists are necessarily wrong, but rather that they ought not be so sure that they are right. In addition to questioning the rationalists' a priori metaphysical assumptions, empiricists question their methodological assumptions. It is not that methodological naturalism should be dropped; rather, it should be used as a tool rather than mandated as a doctrine.

Not surprisingly, rationalists tend to have difficulty with the rejection of their a priori assumptions. For rationalists, their axioms are so self-evident that contrary views seem absurd. "Was the mosquito designed?" they rhetorically ask as if the answer were obviously no. For rationalists, design arguments seem to be avoiding obvious problems that evolution has long since dealt with. "Design," they say, "was disproved by Darwin."

Rationalists also have difficulty with inconclusive or probabilistic interpretations of the evidence. They believe they have the truth, so counterevidences mean little unless they serve to falsify. For Darwin, the existence of incredible complexity in biology was not a problem unless it absolutely falsified evolution: "If it could be demonstrated that any complex organ existed, *which could not possibly have been formed* by numerous, successive, slight modifications, my theory would absolutely break down. But I can find out no such case."[31]

This was hardly a concession. Darwin may sound generous here, allowing that his theory would "absolutely break down," but he set the bar exceedingly high. How can one absolutely prove that the human brain could not have evolved? Biology is full of complexities about whose origin evolution can only speculate. But according to Darwin and the evolutionists, they do not harm evolution, because though they may be improbable, there is no *proof* that they could not have evolved. This remains today the common rebuttal to evidential problems. If evolution can provide an explanation, no matter how speculative and unlikely, then the problem has been deflected.

Drawing upon one-time contingent events, evolutionists can provide explanations for everything we find—even the origin of the DNA code. This leads to the remarkable conclusion, which evolutionists routinely make, that there is no evidence against their theory. This may seem unrealistic given the many problems with the theory we saw in chapters 5 and 6, but for evolutionists it naturally follows from their premises. Descartes and the rationalists crave certainty.

Moderate Empiricism Today

In the twentieth century, astronomers and cosmologists began to scratch out a new and remarkable view of the cosmos. As we saw in chapter 4, the universe seems to be incredibly finely tuned. The strength of gravity, mass and charge of the electron, and dozens of other fundamental constants of nature have values that are just right. The entire universe is balanced on a knife edge, explains physicist Paul Davies, and if any of nature's constants were off even slightly, the result would be total chaos.

Sir Fred Hoyle concluded that a super-intellect has monkeyed with physics, as well as chemistry and biology. Have not the laws of nuclear physics been deliberately designed? The remarkable fact, agrees Stephen Hawking, is that nature's constants seem to have been very finely adjusted to make life possible. The story is a complex one, and we're still trying to understand it all, but the message is clear. The universe is exquisitely tuned. It is not the case that the cosmos is simply a dumb machine or empty box that just happens to be filled with functional structures. Those structures—everything from galaxies and stars to bacteria and molecules—would not even be possible if the workings of nature were not finely tuned.

It would be difficult to imagine a better fulfillment of the prophecy from three centuries ago, declared by thinkers such as Thomas Burnet and Immanuel Kant. Nature and the universe, they claimed, were not insufficient or incapable but rather intricately designed machines. In fact, they argued that precisely these exquisite and unlikely workings of nature lend themselves to a design inference. These thinkers usually took the extreme position: nature was capable not only of sustaining our world but of creating it as well.

Is it possible that naturalistic processes—such as evolution—could have done all this creating? This question has fueled much public debate, and induced strong claims. "Yes, evolution is a fact," and "No, evolution is impossible" are the oft-heard claims. In fact, the question of whether naturalistic processes such as evolution are sufficient receives more attention than it merits. The fact is that while there is much that we have learned, we simply do not have a clear picture of all of natural history. Asking whether evolution has occurred encourages speculation into the unknown rather than a sober evaluation of relevant knowledge. Black-and-white-type questions are not very helpful in gray areas.

What we have learned are many details about naturalistic hypotheses. We now understand much about what is required of nature if evolution occurred. The better question is not, Did evolution occur? but rather, If evolution occurred, what must be true? What magnitude of unlikely contingency must be called upon? How finely tuned must have been the initial conditions? How much serendipity must be invoked? We do not have certainty on natural history, but we do have many answers for questions like these.

This was the approach of Nobel Laureate Francis Crick when at one point he considered directed panspermia—the possibility that the first life on earth was sent here by a distant civilization. What is probably more important than deciding on the veracity of naturalistic theories is deciding on the implications involved. If the naturalistic origin of life on earth is true, then those naturalistic events must have been rather heroic. This much is clear today. Perhaps the initial conditions were just so. Perhaps we need a multiverse to explain such an unlikely event. Or perhaps there are more reasonable naturalistic explanations that have not yet been discovered.

On the other hand, if the origin of life on earth did not occur naturalistically, then we need some alternative explanation such as directed panspermia or special creation. Of course, when naturalistic explanations are reasonably likely, then all other explanations become superfluous and are rejected. But when the science indicates that naturalistic explanations are not likely, then other hypotheses are considered and the explanatory spectrum widens.

Even within the relatively narrow band of naturalism, it is sometimes difficult to establish why one theory is better than another. Theory preference sometimes includes intangible factors. This problem becomes no easier when the scope is widened to include nonnaturalistic explanations such as directed panspermia. Which is the better explanation: first life was placed here by unknown extraterrestrials, or first life arose naturally via unknown intermediates?

When a nonheroic naturalistic explanation is available, then it is the clear choice. When the natural laws that we observe are sufficient to explain a phenomenon, then we must not multiply entities and introduce gratuitous causes in the explanation. This is the principle of parsimony. But as the best naturalistic explanation becomes increasingly unlikely, then the parsimonious scientist begins to consider alternatives. The application of the principle of parsimony becomes more subtle.

The problem now requires a careful weighing of various considerations. We need to consider the science involved. Exactly what are the evidences, and how do they compare with what we know from science? What natural processes are reasonably conceivable, and how close can they come to explaining the data? What additional findings would be required to bridge the gap? These are the sorts of scientific questions that need to be considered.

But in these cases, where naturalism is questionable, the science alone is insufficient. We cannot judge between unknown extraterrestrials and unknown intermediates merely on the basis of scientific details. There are metaphysical, philosophical, theological, and historical questions to consider. These are rich, multifaceted problems that include reasoning from a variety of disciplines. We cannot understand such problems with narrow appeals to just science, or just philosophy, or just theology, or just history. The full range of knowledge ought to be considered.

What I am suggesting here is not new or controversial. Theological naturalists, for instance, routinely make philosophical and theological claims for why only naturalistic solutions should be allowed. But this is merely one school of thought. Other approaches that do not adhere to theological naturalism will not make such a hard restriction.

Obviously it is important to understand the presuppositions of each approach. Rationalist approaches, such as theological naturalism, make strong presuppositions that dictate the results. Science, they say, must be constrained to mechanistic processes. Such axioms provide a strong unifying framework that subsumes both the historical and the experimental sciences. Evolutionists' experimental work is directly dependent on their historical theory. The historical theory, for instance, requires an evolutionary tree, and their experimental work must work within that paradigm. Their historical theory has placed tight restrictions on their experimental work.

Indeed, evolutionists argue that such a framework is necessary. Critics of evolution, they say, must present an alternative theory of equal definitiveness. Rationalists like rationalism. For them, a theory without a strong framework simply does not qualify. But such reasoning is foreign to the moderate empiricist. Empiricists make fewer presuppositions, and where the science has less certainty, their theories are more open ended.

The seventeenth-century moderate empiricists, such as Boyle and Newton, pursued the experimental sciences largely unhindered by axioms or historical science frameworks. Unlike the rationalists, the empiricists were not particularly interested in scientific speculations about the origin of the world. Today this trend continues with design theorists.

A New Framework for Science

For centuries it has been observed that nature appears to have been designed. But rationalism, with its metaphysical axioms, has constrained the sciences to naturalism. This has led to a blind spot, as only naturalistic explanations may be considered. If those naturalistic explanations are correct, then all is well. But today's rationalism has proclaimed them to be correct by fiat. This is metaphysical certainty, not scientific certainty.

Moderate empiricism provides an alternative approach. The intelligent design theory is a typical example of empiricist thinking. Unfortunately, the criticism of intelligent design has mostly come from rationalism and theological naturalism. Design theorists must be employing objectionable axioms. Are they not bringing miracles into science? Are they not forcing religion into science and using it as a theistic proof? Are they not making science capricious and arbitrary? Is this not a science stopper?

Such criticisms reveal more about the critics than about intelligent design. Intelligent design has not stepped into a God-of-the-gaps blunder for the simple reason that it is not predicating religious faith on scientific results. The evidence for design is overwhelming. Rather than rejecting the obvious, intelligent design recognizes the evidence and pursues explanations. No a priori assumptions are made about what solutions are and are not allowed. This is certainly not a science stopper, and we can be glad that Newton and the early moderate empiricists did not think this way.

Intelligent design cuts the strong tie between the historical and experimental sciences that rationalism requires. It is mainly interested in pursuing the experimental sciences without a priori assumptions about what is the right answer. Unfortunately, there is a common misunderstanding that intelligent design is opposed to all naturalistic explanations. Nothing could be further from the truth. Intelligent design is opposed, however, to simple-minded, dogmatic blinders when we are dealing with complex problems. We should not assume we know the kind of answers science must produce when there is much uncertainty. The world may have arisen by any of a variety of means, and there is little to be gained by prematurely narrowing the choices.

This leads to a wide range of scientific research. In biology, for instance, the species can be analyzed without the researcher necessarily assuming that they evolved from each other. Evolution may be the best explanation, or it may not be.

Design theory also leads to a new way of looking at how nature works. In what ways are nature's constants and the natural laws themselves fine-tuned? How is it, for instance, that nature produces uniform action and distinct types and yet is often so unpredictable? And in what ways are nature's creations fine-tuned? We are beginning to see patterns for which naturalists would not think to look. Intelligent design is not about proving religion. It is about analyzing the workings of nature without religious constraint.

Notes

Preface

1. Alfred N. Whitehead, *Science and the Modern World* (New York: Macmillan, 1925), 49.

Chapter 2 The Revolution That Wasn't

1. Sachiko Kusukawa, "Bacon's Classification of Knowledge," in *Bacon*, ed. Markku Peltonen (Cambridge: Cambridge University Press, 1996), 53.

2. Bacon did not always adhere closely to the empiricism he so tirelessly promoted. In the area of cosmology, Bacon indulged in seemingly uncharacteristic speculation. He was interested in the problems of celestial motion and the distribution of matter in the universe. His ideas would be strange to a modern reader but not to a contemporary. More important, though, Bacon introduced unsupported assertions, such as that nature distributes matter by separating rare bodies from gross, to explain how the earth and celestial bodies are arranged. This sounds more like the sort of preconception he opposed than his clean-slate approach. As one historian puts it, "There is a doubleness to his philosophical enterprise." See Graham Rees, "Bacon's Speculative Philosophy," in *Bacon*, ed. Peltonen, 121, 133.

3. John C. Briggs, "Bacon's Science and Religion," in *Bacon*, ed. Peltonen, 172.

4. Ibid., 174.

5. Kusukawa, "Bacon's Classification of Knowledge," in *Bacon*, ed. Peltonen, 61.

6. Briggs, "Bacon's Science and Religion," in *Bacon*, ed. Peltonen, 178.

7. Ibid., 176.

8. Bacon, quoted in Norman F. Cantor and Peter L. Klein, *Seventeenth-Century Rationalism: Bacon and Descartes* (Waltham, MA: Blaisdell, 1969), 29.

9. René Descartes, quoted in Desmond Clarke, "Descartes' Philosophy of Science and the Scientific Revolution," in *Descartes*, ed. John Cottingham (Cambridge: Cambridge University Press, 1992), 266.

10. Ibid., 269–70.

11. Ibid., 268.

12. See, for example, John Hedley Brooke, *Science and Religion: Some Historical Perspectives* (Cambridge: Cambridge University Press, 1991), 117.

13. William B. Ashworth, "Christianity and the Mechanistic Universe," in *When Science and Christianity Meet*, ed. David C. Lindberg and Ronald L. Numbers (Chicago: University of Chicago Press, 2003), 61–84; John Hedley Brooke, *Science and Religion: Some Historical Perspectives* (Cambridge: Cambridge University Press, 1991), 117–43.

14. For example, historian Stephen Brush writes: "Thus a major new feature of post-1750 cosmogony was the rejection of theological assumptions about how and when the world was created." Stephen G. Brush, *Nebulous Earth: The Origin of the Solar System and the Core of the Earth from Laplace to Jeffreys* (Cambridge: Cambridge University Press, 1996), 5.

15. Thomas Burnet, quoted in Stephen Jay Gould, *Ever since Darwin: Reflections in Natural History* (New York: W. W. Norton, 1973), 141–46.

16. Isaac Newton, *The Principia* (1687), trans. Andrew Motte (Amherst, NY: Prometheus, 1995), 440.

17. Edwin A. Burtt, *The Metaphysical Foundations of Modern Science* (Garden City, NY: Doubleday Anchor, 1954), 296–98.

18. Ashworth, "Christianity and the Mechanistic Universe," 83–84, and Thomas H. Broman, "Matter, Force, and the Christian Worldview in the Enlightenment," 91, in *When Science and Christianity Meet*, ed. David C. Lindberg and Ronald L. Numbers (Chicago: University of Chicago Press, 2003).

19. Brush, *Nebulous Earth*, 17.

20. John Ray, *The Wisdom of God Manifested in the Works of the Creation*, 7th ed., corrected (1717; reprint New York: Arno, 1977), 51.

21. Immanuel Kant, *Universal Natural History and Theory of Heaven* (1755), trans. Ian C. Johnston, available at www.mala.bc.ca/~johnstoi/kant2e.htm#sect1.

22. Erasmus Darwin, *Zoonomia: or, The Laws of Organic Life* (London: J. Johnson, 1794), 1:509; quoted in George B. Dysan, "Darwin in Kansas," *Science* 285 (1999): 1355.

23. John Playfair, quoted in Charles C. Gillispie, *Genesis and Geology* (Cambridge: Harvard University Press, 1951), 76.

24. Neal C. Gillespie, *Charles Darwin and the Problem of Creation* (Chicago: University of Chicago Press, 1979), 59.

25. Robert Chambers, quoted in Gillispie, *Genesis and Geology*, 155.

26. Charles Kingsley, quoted in George L. Murphy, *The Cosmos in the Light of the Cross* (Harrisburg, PA: Trinity Press International, 2003), 119.

27. James C. Livingstone, *Modern Christian Thought: From the Enlightenment to Vatican II* (New York: Macmillan, 1971), 4, 13.

28. Ibid., 36.

29. A. C. McGiffert, *Protestant Thought before Kant* (New York: Harper and Brothers, 1961), 212.

30. Ibid., 223–4.

31. Kant, *Universal Natural History*.

32. Ibid.

33. The problem of evil is a theological argument because it requires premises about God. It does not follow from the problem of evil that the world would be free of evil. Based on the premise that God is all-powerful, all-knowing, and all-good, the world may or may not be free of evil. Additional rationalistic axioms about God are needed, but such axioms are usually left unspoken.

34. David Hume, *Dialogues concerning Natural Religion*, quoted in Anders Jeffner, *Butler and Hume on Religion* (Stockholm: Aktiebolaget Trychmans, 1966), 150.

35. Thomas Burnet, quoted in Keith Thomson, *Before Darwin: Reconciling God and Nature* (New Haven, CT: Yale University Press, 2005), 145.

36. Ray, *Wisdom of God*, 51.

37. Kenneth R. Miller, *Finding Darwin's God* (New York: Cliff Street, 1999), 102.

38. Francisco J. Ayala, "Evolution in Kansas: Disservice to Education, Science, and Religion," *Science Teacher*, February 2000.

39. Francisco Ayala, quoted in Gary Robbins, "Hard Science, Firm Beliefs," *Orange County Register*, December 16, 2002.

40. Historian Robert M. Burns comments that almost every English theologian, philosopher, or even simply man of letters of the period made some contribution to this early-eighteenth-century English debate on miracles. See Robert M. Burns, *The Great Debate on Miracles: From Joseph Glanvill to David Hume* (London: Associated University Press, 1981), 10.

41. Thomas Wollaston, quoted in John Earman, *Hume's Abject Failure: The Argument against Miracles* (Oxford: Oxford University Press, 2000), 16.

42. Peter Annet, quoted in ibid., 19.

43. Burns, *Great Debate on Miracles*, 85.

44. Ibid., 86.

45. Annet, quoted in ibid., 87.

46. Ibid., 19.

47. Ibid., 20.

48. As Earman writes,

> In "Of Miracles," Hume pretends to stand on philosophical high ground, hurl-
> ing down thunderbolts against miracle stories. The thunderbolts are supposed
> to issue from general principles about inductive inference and the credibility
> of eyewitness testimony. But when these principles are made explicit and
> examined under the lens of Bayesianism, they are found to be either vapid,
> specious, or at variance with actual scientific practice. When Hume leaves the
> philosophical high ground to evaluate particular miracle stories, his discussion
> is superficial and certainly does not do justice to the extensive and vigorous
> debate about miracles that had been raging for several decades in Britain. He
> was able to create the illusion of a powerful argument by maintaining ambigui-
> ties in his claims against miracles, by the use of forceful prose and confident
> pronouncements, and by liberal doses of sarcasm and irony.

See Earman, *Hume's Abject Failure*, 70.

49. Ibid., 71.

50. See for example, Robert B. Mullin, "Science, Miracles, and the Prayer-Gauge
Debate," in *When Science and Christianity Meet*, ed. David C. Lindberg and Ronald L.
Numbers (Chicago: University of Chicago Press, 2003), 203–24.

51. Gillispie, *Genesis and Geology*, 195–96.

52. Ibid., 190.

53. See, for example, Mullin, "Science, Miracles, and the Prayer-Gauge Debate,"
207.

54. Baden Powell, quoted in Gillespie, *Charles Darwin and the Problem of Creation*, 151.

55. Joseph Le Conte, *Evolution: Its Nature, Its Evidences, and Its Relation to Religious Thought*, 2nd ed. (New York: D. Appleton, 1891), 65–66.

56. George Romanes and Karl von Nägeli, quoted in Gillespie, *Charles Darwin
and the Problem of Creation*, 151.

57. Pierre Teilhard de Chardin, quoted in Theodosius Dobzhansky, *Mankind
Evolving* (New Haven, CT: Yale University Press, 1962), 347.

58. Richard Bentley accused Thomas Burnet of atheism, as we shall see in chapter 3. Geologists accused of James Hutton of atheism. See Gillispie, *Genesis and Geology*, 75. Charles Hodge accused Darwin of atheism. See Charles Hodge, *What Is Darwinism?* (1874), ed. Mark Noll and David Livingstone (Grand Rapids: Baker, 1994). And today it is not uncommon for evolutionists to be accused of atheism.

59. David Hume, *Dialogues concerning Natural Religion*, pt. 2, www.anselm.edu/homepage/dbanach/dnr.htm.

60. Gillispie, *Genesis and Geology*, xxviii.

61. See, for example, William B. Ashworth, "Christianity and the Mechanistic Universe," in *When Science and Christianity Meet*, ed. David C. Lindberg and Ronald L. Numbers (Chicago: University of Chicago Press, 2003), 72–73.

Chapter 3 Science's Blind Spot

1. Stephen G. Brush, *Nebulous Earth: The Origin of the Solar System and the Core of the Earth from Laplace to Jeffreys* (Cambridge: Cambridge University Press, 1996), 15.

2. Today the story is more complex. Chaos theory, quantum mechanics, black holes, and other twentieth-century discoveries of ambiguity have brought uncertainty even into Laplace's world. It appears that a Laplacean computer is not merely impractical but not even possible in principle.

3. Brush, *Nebulous Earth*, 42–43.

4. Charles Darwin, *On the Origin of Species*, 6th ed. (1872; reprint London: Collier Macmillan, 1962), 484–85.

5. For example, Douglas Futuyma writes, "An observation is accepted as a scientific 'fact' only if it can be repeated by other individuals who follow the same methods." Douglas J. Futuyma, *Science on Trial: The Case for Evolution* (New York: Pantheon, 1982), 166.

6. This is not to say there are no repeatability challenges in the experimental sciences. In fact, technically it is impossible to repeat an observation because of the many uncertainties and random variables in any given experiment. Both the experimental process itself and the measurements cannot be exactly repeated. Often these uncertainties are not significant, but sometimes they are. Single particle experiments, for example, are often unique and not repeatable. Hopefully these random effects, when significant, can be overcome through the making of additional experiments.

7. Ernst Mayr, "Darwin's Influence on Modern Thought," *Scientific American*, July 2000, 80.

8. Victor Stenger, "Is the Universe Fine-Tuned for Us?" in *Why Intelligent Design Fails: A Scientific Critique of the New Creationism*, ed. Matt Young and Taner Edis (New Brunswick, NJ: Rutgers University Press, 2004), 182.

9. J. T. Trevorsa and D. L. Abel, "Chance and Necessity Do Not Explain the Origin of Life," *Cell Biology International* 28 (2004): 729–39.

10. Thomas S. Kuhn, *The Structure of Scientific Revolutions* (Chicago: University of Chicago Press, 1962).

11. Maitland A. Edey and Donald C. Johanson, *Blueprints: Solving the Mystery of Evolution* (Boston: Little, Brown, 1989), 291.

12. Thomas Burnet quoted in Keith Thomson, *Before Darwin: Reconciling God and Nature* (New Haven, CT: Yale University Press, 2005), 223.

13. See Charles Hodge, *What Is Darwinism?* (1874), ed. Mark Noll and David Livingstone (Grand Rapids: Baker, 1994), and Alvin Plantinga, "Methodological Naturalism?" *Origins and Design* 18, no. 1 (1997), available at www.arn.org/docs/odesign/od181/methnat181.htm.

14. Plantinga, "Methodological Naturalism?"

Chapter 4 A God in the Machine

1. Isaac Newton, *The Principia* (1687), trans. Andrew Motte (Amherst, NY: Prometheus, 1995), 315.

2. Marjorie Hope Nicolson, "Literary Attitudes toward Mountains," available at http://etext.lib.virginia.edu/cgi-local/DHI/dhi.cgi?id=dv3–31.

3. "In 1692 Richard Bentley delivered the first Boyle Lecture, *The Folly and Unreasonableness of Atheism Demonstrated from the Origin and Frame of the World*. Men like Burnet, he says in effect, think that mountain, valley, ocean are deformity, ruin or fortuitous concourse of atoms rather than what they are—works of Divine artifice. 'They would have the vast body of a planet to be as elegant as a factitious globe represents it.'" See ibid.

4. Ibid.

5. Daniel Bernoulli, "Physical and Astronomical Researches on the Problem Proposed for the Second Time by the Academie Royale des Sciences de Paris" (1734), available at http://cerebro.xu.edu/math/Sources/DanBernoulli/bern_comets.pdf.

6. Ibid.

7. Immanuel Kant, *Universal Natural History and Theory of Heaven* (1755), trans. Ian C. Johnston, available at www.mala.bc.ca/~johnstoi/kant2e.htm#sect1.

8. Ibid.

9. Ibid.

10. George Louis Leclerc, comte de Buffon, *Proofs of the Theory of the Earth*, article 1, *Of the Formation of Planets*, available at http://faculty.njcu.edu/fmoran/vol1art2.htm.

11. The Nebular Hypothesis had earlier been proposed by Kant, but there is no evidence Laplace knew of Kant's theory. See Stephen G. Brush, *Nebulous Earth: The Origin of the Solar System and the Core of the Earth from Laplace to Jeffreys* (Cambridge: Cambridge University Press, 1996), 22.

12. Pierre Laplace, quoted in ibid., 22.

13. Brush, *Nebulous Earth*, 21.

14. For details of this sequence, see ibid., 134–36.

15. Ibid., 4.

16. Keay Davidson, "Heated Debate on Formation of Solar System: Theorist Believes Nine Planets Created out of Chaos, Not Calm," *San Francisco Chronicle*, June 17, 2002.

17. Mark Peplow, "The Triple Sunset That Should Not Exist," *Nature* 436 (2005), available at www.nature.com/news/2005/050711/full/050711–6.html; Macicj Konacki, "An Extrasolar Giant Planet in a Close Triple-Star System," *Nature* 436 (2005): 230–33.

18. Davidson, "Heated Debate on Formation of Solar System."

19. Edward Belbruno and J. Richard Gott, "Where Did the Moon Come From?" (2005), available at http://arxiv.org/abs/astro-ph/0405372.

20. "Surprise Discovery of Highly Developed Structure in the Young Universe," *ScienceDaily*, March 2005, available at www.sciencedaily.com/releases/2005/03/050309120108.htm.

21. "Astronomers See Era of Rapid Galaxy Formation," *BrightSurf*, January 2004, available at www.brightsurf.com/news/jan_04/NSF_news_010904.php.

22. Edward Rothstein, "Finding the Universal Laws That Are There, Waiting . . . " *New York Times*, January 10, 2004.

23. Fred C. Adams and Gregory Laughlin, *The Five Ages of the Universe: Inside the Physics of Eternity* (New York: Free Press, 1999), 199, 201.

24. W. R. Stoeger, G. F. R. Ellis, and U. Kirchner, "Multiverses and Cosmology: Philosophical Issues" (2004), available at http://arxiv.org/abs/astro-ph/0407329.

25. *Scientific American*, May 2003, cover.

Chapter 5 Nature's Innovative Power

1. Benoit De Maillet, *Telliamed: Or, Discourses between an Indian Philosopher and a French Missionary, on the Diminution of the Sea, the Formation of the Earth, the Origin of Men and Animals, and Other Curious Subjects, Relating to Natural History and Philosophy* (orig. 1750; Champaign: University of Illinois Press, 1968).

2. John Hedley Brooke, *Science and Religion: Some Historical Perspectives* (Cambridge: Cambridge University Press, 1991), 241–43.

3. As Douglas Futuyma writes, "It is not clear what led Lamarck to his uncompromising belief in evolution." Douglas J. Futuyma, *Science on Trial: The Case for Evolution* (New York: Pantheon, 1982), 28.

4. Adrian Desmond and James Moore, *Darwin* (New York: W. W. Norton, 1991), 34–40.

5. Charles Darwin, quoted at www.ucmp.berkeley.edu/history/lamarck.html.

6. Auguste Comte, quoted in John C. Greene, *Science, Ideology, and World View* (Berkeley: University of California Press, 1981), 63–66.

7. Janet Browne, *The Secular Ark: Studies in the History of Biogeography* (New Haven, CT: Yale University Press, 1983), 167.

8. Michael Ruse, *Darwinism Defended* (Reading, MA: Addison-Wesley, 1982), 3.

9. For the problem of how complex designs arose via evolution, Darwin shifted the burden to the skeptic: "If it could be demonstrated that any complex organ existed, which could not possibly have been formed by numerous, successive, slight modifications, my theory would absolutely break down. But I can find out no such case." Charles Darwin, *On the Origin of Species*, 6th ed. (1872; reprint London: Collier Macmillan, 1962), 182.

10. Browne, *Secular Ark*, 169.

11. Darwin, *On the Origin of Species*, 437.

12. Gavin de Beer, *Atlas of Evolution* (London: Nelson, 1964), 44.

13. Carl Zimmer, *Evolution* (New York: HarperCollins, 2001), 124.

14. "There's only one inescapable conclusion which is: If all of these branches have these genes, then you have to go to the base of that, which is the last common ancestor of all animals, and you deduce it must have had these genes." Sean Carroll, quoted in Discovery Institute, *Getting the Facts Straight: A Viewer's Guide to PBS's Evolution* (Seattle: Discovery Institute, 2001), 24.

15. Stephen C. Stearns and Rolf F. Hoekstra, *Evolution: An Introduction* (Oxford: Oxford University Press, 2000), 127.

16. S. Gilbert, J. Opitz, and R. Raff, "Resynthesizing Evolutionary and Developmental Biology," *Developmental Biology* 173 (1996): 357–72.

17. For example, see Stephen Jay Gould, *The Structure of Evolutionary Theory*, (Cambridge, MA: Belknap, 2002), 579, 582.

18. D. Irwin, "Macroevolution Is More Than Repeated Rounds of Microevolution," *Evolutionary Development* 2 (2000): 61–62.

19. For example, Julian Huxley describes one example from fruit fly experiments:

> Finally, we have the curious fact that the harmful effects of mutant genes may automatically be selected back toward normality. For instance, the so-called

eyeless mutant of the famous fruit fly, Drosophila, at its first appearance had no or small eyes, and was less healthy and in general less capable of survival than normal wild-type flies. But after a pure eyeless strain had been bred for eight or ten generations, both its health and vigor and its eyes were almost normal. Any odd mutant genes already present in small numbers in the strain, which reduced the harmful effects of the eyeless mutation, automatically multiplied at the expense of those which did not. Natural selection, in effect, provided a genetic servo-mechanism to regulate the mutant back toward normality in its effects. (Julian Huxley, *Evolution in Action* [New York: Harper and Row, 1953], 40)

20. D. Leipe, L. Aravind, and E. V. Koonin, "Did DNA Replication Evolve Twice Independently?" *Nucleic Acids Research* 27 (1999): 3389–401.

21. G. B. Johnson and P. H. Raven, *Biology* (New York: Holt, Rinehart and Winston, 2004), 286.

22. Gavin de Beer, *Homology: An Unsolved Problem* (Oxford: Oxford University Press, 1971).

23. A. G. Jacobson and A. K. Sater, "Features of Embryonic Induction," *Development* 104 (1988): 341–59. As Pere Alberch notes, examples of similar structures, supposed to have been inherited from a common ancestor, developing from dissimilar initial states or different development pathways are "the rule rather than the exception." See P. Alberch, "Problems with the Interpretation of Developmental Sequences," *Systematic Zoology* 34 (1985): 51. And Brian Hall writes, "Because there are so many examples of homologous structures arising from nonhomologous development processes, I believe homology can no longer retain its historical links to shared embryonic development." Brian Hall, "Homology and Embryonic Development," *Evolutionary Biology* 28 (1995): 1.

24. De Beer, *Homology*, 16.

25. Two plant species in the nightshade family have quite similar anther cones in their flowers, but their developmental pathways are different. Commenting on this, Günter Thebien writes: "Structures that occur in closely related organisms and that look the same are usually considered to be homologous—their similarity is taken to arise from their common ancestry. Common sense suggests that the more complex such structures are, the less likely they are to have evolved independently and the more valuable they should be for studying systematics. But what if obviously identical organs have arisen through two mutually exclusive developmental routes?" Günter Thebien, "Developmental Genetics: Bittersweet Evolution," *Nature* 428 (2004): 813.

26. Ibid.

Chapter 6 When Predictions Go Wrong

1. Charles Darwin, *On the Origin of Species*, 6th ed. (1872; reprint London: Collier Macmillan, 1962), 26.

2. Anna Gosline, "Birds of a Feather Not Related to Each Other," *New Scientist*, December 2004, available at www.newscientist.com/article.ns?id=dn6762.

3. Roxanne Khamsi, "Similarity of Construction Shows 'Convergent Evolution' Applies to Behaviour," *Nature*, November 2004, available at www.nature.com/news/2004/041101/full/041101–4.html; T. Blackledge and R. Gillespie, "Convergent Evolution of Behavior in an Adaptive Radiation of Hawaiian Web-Building Spiders," *Proceedings of the National Academy of Sciences USA* 101 (2004): 16228.

4. See, for example, Simon Conway Morris, *Life's Solutions: Inevitable Humans in a Lonely Universe* (Cambridge: Cambridge University Press, 2003).

5. Carl Woese, "The Universal Ancestor," *Proceedings of the National Academy of Sciences USA* 95 (1998): 6854.

6. Ibid.; also W. Ford Doolittle, "The Nature of the Universal Ancestor and the Evolution of the Proteome," *Current Opinion in Structural Biology* 10 (2000): 355–58.

7. Arthur W. Lindsey, *Principles of Organic Evolution* (St. Louis: C. V. Mosby, 1952), 120.

8. Alok Jha, "Human Brain Result of 'Extraordinarily Fast' Evolution," *Guardian*, December 29, 2004; S. Dorus, "Accelerated Evolution of Nervous System Genes in the Origin of *Homo sapiens*," *Cell* 119 (2004): 1027–40.

9. T. H. Huxley, quoted in Stephen Jay Gould, "The Episodic Nature of Evolutionary Change," in *The Panda's Thumb* (New York: W. W. Norton, 1980), 179.

10. Charles Darwin, quoted in ibid., 181.

11. Scott F. Gilbert, Grace A. Loredo, Alla Brukman, and Ann C. Burke, "Morphogenesis of the Turtle Shell: The Development of a Novel Structure in Tetrapod Evolution," *Evolution and Development* 3 (2001): 47–58.

12. T. S. Kemp, *Fossils and Evolution* (Oxford: Oxford University Press, 1999), 16.

13. "Pack Rat Middens Give Unique View on Evolution and Climate Change in Past Million Years," *ScienceDaily*, October 2003, available at www.sciencedaily.com/releases/2003/10/031031062755.htm.

14. D. Y. Huang , J. Y. Chen, J. Vannier, and J. I. Saiz Salinas, "Early Cambrian Sipunculan Worms from Southwest China," *Proceedings Biological Sciences* 271 (2004): 1671–76.

15. "Army Ants Have Defied Evolution for 100 Million Years," *Newswise*, May 2003, available at www.newswise.com/p/articles/view/?id=ARMYANT.CNS; S. G. Brady, "Evolution of the Army Ant Syndrome: The Origin and Long-Term Evolutionary

Stasis of a Complex of Behavioral and Reproductive Adaptations," *Proceedings of the National Academy of Sciences USA* 100 (2003): 6575–79.

16. M. A. Gandolfo, K. C. Nixon, and W. L. Crepet, "Cretaceous Flowers of Nymphaeaceae and Implications for Complex Insect Entrapment Pollination Mechanisms in Early Angiosperms," *Proceedings of the National Academy of Sciences USA* 101 (2004): 8056–60.

17. For example, the celebrated reptile-mammalian transition in fact has significant gaps and convergences. It requires, for instance, the independent evolution of several complex, unique mammalian cranial and dental features. See T. Martin and Z. Luo, "Homoplasy in the Mammalian Ear," *Science* 307 (2005): 861.

18. See, for example, Julie E. Horvath, et. al., "Punctuated duplication seeding events during the evolution of human chromosome 2p11," *Genome Research* 15 (2005): 914–27.

19. M. Barbulescu et al., "A HERV-K Provirus in Chimpanzees, Bonobos, and Gorillas, but Not Humans," *Current Biology* 11 (2001): 779–83.

20. W. Johnson and J. Coffin, "Constructing Primate Phylogenies from Ancient Retrovirus Sequences," *Proceedings of the National Academy of Sciences USA* 96 (1999): 10254–60.

21. National Academy of Sciences, *Science and Creationism: A View from the National Academy of Sciences*, 2nd ed. (Washington, DC: National Academy Press, 1999), 19.

22. Cornelius G. Hunter, *Darwin's Proof: The Triumph of Religion over Science* (Grand Rapids: Brazos, 2003), 50–53.

23. T. Gura, "Bones, Molecules . . . or Both?" *Nature* 406 (2000): 230–33.

24. For example, see P. Lockhart and S. Cameron, "Trees for Bees," *Trends in Ecology and Evolution* 16 (2001): 84–88.

25. Michael Balter, "Morphologists Learn to Live with Molecular Upstarts," *Science* 276 (1997): 1034.

26. J. Raymond et al., "Whole-Genome Analysis of Photosynthetic Prokaryotes," *Science* 298 (2002): 1616–19.

27. A. Feduccia, "'Big Bang' for Tertiary Birds?" *Trends in Ecology and Evolution* 18 (2003): 175.

28. W. de Jong, "Molecules Remodel the Mammalian Tree," *Trends in Ecology and Evolution* 13 (1998): 270–75.

29. M. Whiting, S. Bradler, and T. Maxwell, "Loss and Recovery of Wings in Stick Insects," *Nature* 421 (2003): 264–67.

30. Hunter, *Darwin's Proof*, 57.

31. Woese, "Universal Ancestor," 6854.

32. E. Bapteste et al., "Do Orthologous Gene Phylogenies Really Support Tree-Thinking?" *BMC Evolutionary Biology* 5 (2005): 33.

33. D. Penny, L. Foulds, and M. Hendy, "Testing the Theory of Evolution by Comparing Phylogenetic Trees Constructed from Five Different Protein Sequences," *Nature* 297 (1982): 200.

34. V. Daubin, H. Ochman, "Bacterial Genomes as New Gene Homes: The Genealogy of ORFans in E. coli," *Genome Research* 14 (2004): 1036–42.

35. S. Agarwal and M. Behe, "Non-conservative Mutations Are Well Tolerated in the Globular Region of Yeast Histone H4," *Journal of Molecular Biology* 255 (1996): 401–11.

36. Helen Pearson, " 'Junk' DNA Reveals Vital Role," *Nature*, May 2004, available at www.nature.com/nsu/040503/040503–9.html.

Chapter 7 Inherit the Wind All Over Again

1. See, for example, William B. Ashworth, "Christianity and the Mechanistic Universe," in *When Science and Christianity Meet*, ed. David C. Lindberg and Ronald L. Numbers (Chicago: University of Chicago Press, 2003) 61–84; John Hedley Brooke, *Science and Religion: Some Historical Perspectives* (Cambridge: Cambridge University Press, 1991); Guillermo Gonzalez, Jay Richards, *The Privileged Planet: How Our Place in the Cosmos Is Designed for Discovery* (Washington, DC: Regnery Publishing, 2004); Alister E. McGrath, *Dawkins' God: Genes, Memes, and the Meaning of Life* (Oxford: Blackwell, 2005), 140–46; Colin A. Russell, "The Conflict of Science and Religion," in *Science & Religion*, ed. Gary B. Ferngren (Baltimore: Johns Hopkins University Press, 2002), 3–12; David B. Wilson, "The Historiography of Science and Religion," in *Science & Religion*, ed. Gary B. Ferngren (Baltimore: Johns Hopkins University Press, 2002), 13–29.

2. See, for example, David C. Lindberg and Ronald L. Numbers, introduction to *When Science and Christianity Meet*, 1–2; and David N. Livingstone, "Re-placing Darwinism and Christianity," in *When Science and Christianity Meet*, 183–202.

3. Andrew D. White, introduction to *History of the Warfare of Science with Theology in Christendom* (New York: D. Appleton, 1896), available at http://cscs.umich.edu/~crshalizi/White/introduction.html.

4. Ibid.

5. Charles Darwin, *On the Origin of Species*, 6th ed. (1872; reprint London: Collier Macmillan, 1962), 435.

6. Charles Darwin, quoted in John C. Greene, *Science, Ideology, and World View* (Berkeley: University of California Press, 1981), 52.

7. Neal C. Gillespie, *Charles Darwin and the Problem of Creation* (Chicago: University of Chicago Press, 1979), 32–33.

8. Joseph Le Conte, *Evolution: Its Nature, Its Evidences, and Its Relation to Religious Thought*, 2nd ed. (New York: D. Appleton, 1891), 65–66.

9. Thomas Huxley, 1906, quoted in Antony Flew, *Darwinian Evolution*, 2nd ed. (London: Transaction, 1997), 19.

10. John Rennie, "15 Answers to Creationist Nonsense," *Scientific American*, July, 2002.

11. John E. Jones, *Kitzmiller v. Dover Area School District*, 04-CV-2688, WL 578974 (M.D. Pa. 2005): 66.

12. Ibid., 22. Here Jones was reaffirming the 1982 *McLean* v. *Arkansas Board of Education* decision.

13. Ibid., 66.

14. Ibid., 64.

15. Ibid., 137.

16. Keith Thomson, *Before Darwin: Reconciling God and Nature* (New Haven, CT: Yale University Press, 2005), 92.

17. Ibid., 94.

18. Compare this with the view of the ancient Hebrews: God created the species with more in mind than material performance or pleasing our sentiment. He created the donkey, for instance, to be obstinate (Job 39).

19. Thomson, *Before Darwin*, 92.

20. Ibid., 100–106, 217.

21. Ibid., 104.

22. Ibid., 106.

23. Ibid., 106–7.

24. See chap. 8 in this volume, and see Cornelius G. Hunter, *Darwin's God: Evolution and the Problem of Evil* (Grand Rapids: Brazos, 2001).

25. Thomson, *Before Darwin*, 239.

26. G. B. Johnson and P. H. Raven, *Biology* (New York: Holt, Rinehart, and Winston, 2004), 280.

27. Theories are not proved by successful predictions. This is the fallacy of affirming the consequent.

28. Theodosius Dobzhansky, "Nothing in Biology Makes Sense Except in the Light of Evolution," *American Biology Teacher* 35 (1973): 125–29.

29. Bruce Alberts et al., *Molecular Biology of the Cell*, 3rd ed. (New York: Garland, 1994), 241.

Chapter 8 Theological Naturalism

1. Charles Darwin, *On the Origin of Species*, 6th ed. (1872; reprint London: Collier Macmillan, 1962), 483–84.

2. Ibid., 477.

3. Kenneth R. Miller, *Finding Darwin's God* (New York: Cliff Street, 1999), 102.

4. Ibid., 238.

5. Ibid.

6. Howard Van Till, "The Fully Gifted Creation," in *Three Views on Creation and Evolution*, edited by J. P. Moreland and John M. Reynolds (Grand Rapids: Zondervan, 1999), 187.

7. Ian G. Barbour, quoted in Stephen J. Lee, "Science and Religion," *Grand Forks Herald*, July 31, 2004.

8. Ian G. Barbour, *When Science Meets Religion* (New York: HarperCollins, 2000), 112.

9. George L. Murphy, *The Cosmos in the Light of the Cross* (Harrisburg, PA: Trinity Press International, 2003), 78–79.

10. Ted Peters and Martinez Hewlett, *Evolution from Creation to New Creation: Conflict, Conversation, and Convergence* (Nashville: Abingdon, 2003), 152.

11. John Polkinghorne, *Belief in God in an Age of Science* (New Haven, CT: Yale Nota Bene, 1998), 13.

12. Ibid.

13. John F. Haught, *Deeper Than Darwin: The Prospect for Religion in the Age of Evolution* (Cambridge, MA: Westview, 2003), 86.

14. Paul Nelson, "The Role of Theology in Current Evolutionary Reasoning," *Biology and Philosophy* 11 (1996): 493–517.

15. Stephen Jay Gould, "The Panda's Thumb," in *The Panda's Thumb* (New York: W. W. Norton, 1980), 20–21.

16. Darwin, *On the Origin of Species*, 73–74.

17. Ibid., 384.

18. Ibid.

19. Ibid., 143.

20. Ibid., 398.

21. Ibid., 401.

22. Ibid., 402.

23. Ibid., 405.

24. Ibid., 153.

25. Ibid., 156.

26. Ibid., 177–78.

27. Ibid., 192.

28. Ibid.

29. Ibid., 434–35.

30. Ibid., 164–65.

31. Ibid., 196–97.

32. Ibid., 469–70, 475–76.

33. Ibid., 441.

34. Ibid., 196–97.

35. Ibid., 181–82.

36. Cornelius G. Hunter, *Darwin's God: Evolution and the Problem of Evil* (Grand Rapids: Brazos, 2001).

37. Charles C. Gillispie, *Genesis and Geology* (Cambridge, MA: Harvard University Press, 1951), 209.

38. William Buckland, quoted in Steven Jay Gould, "Nonmoral Nature," in *Hen's Teeth and Horse's Toes* (New York: W. W. Norton, 1983), 33.

39. William Buckland, quoted in Gillispie, *Genesis and Geology*, 1951), 201.

40. William Kirby, quoted in Gould, "Nonmoral Nature," 40.

41. Darwin, *On the Origin of Species*, 469–70.

42. The quote is from Donald Fleming; see David N. Livingstone, "Re-placing Darwinism and Christianity," in *When Science and Christianity Meet*, edited by David C. Lindberg and Ronald L. Numbers (Chicago: University of Chicago Press, 2003), 188.

43. Charles Darwin, quoted in Gould, "Nonmoral Nature," 41–42.

44. Livingstone, "Re-placing Darwinism and Christianity," 189.

45. Haught, *Deeper Than Darwin*, 103.

46. Peters and Hewlett, *Evolution from Creation to New Creation*, 21.

47. Haught, *Deeper Than Darwin*, 35.

48. Murphy, *Cosmos in the Light of the Cross*, 81. Note that Murphy's term *existentialism* does not refer to the philosophy of existentialism.

Chapter 9 Moderate Empiricism

1. A. F. Chalmers, *What Is This Thing Called Science?* 2nd ed. (Indianapolis: Hackett, 1982), 102.

2. See John C. Greene, *Science, Ideology, and World View* (Berkeley: University of California Press, 1981).

3. Andrew Dickson White, 1896, quoted in Douglas J. Futuyma, *Science on Trial: The Case for Evolution* (New York: Pantheon, 1982), 3.

4. Joseph Le Conte, *Evolution: Its Nature, Its Evidences, and Its Relation to Religious Thought*, 2nd ed. (New York: D. Appleton, 1891), 65–66.

5. Pierre Teilhard de Chardin, quoted in Theodosius Dobzhansky, *Mankind Evolving* (New Haven, CT: Yale University Press, 1962), 347.

6. Ashley Montagu, back cover of Futuyma, *Science on Trial*.

7. Ernst Mayr, *What Evolution Is* (New York: BasicBooks, 2001), 264.

8. Mark Ridley, *Evolution* (Boston: Blackwell Scientific, 1993), 46–58.

9. George C. Williams, *The Pony Fish's Glow: And Other Clues to Plan and Purpose in Nature* (New York: BasicBooks, 1997), 5–6.

10. Ibid., 2, 9.

11. Ibid., 134, 153–54.

12. Futuyma, *Science on Trial*, 198–99.

13. Ibid., 62, 127, 198–99.

14. Ibid., 200–2.

15. Kenneth R. Miller, *Finding Darwin's God* (New York: Cliff Street, 1999), 97, 100–103.

16. Martin Gardner, "Denying Darwin," *Commentary*, September 1996, 16.

17. Stephen Jay Gould, "The Panda's Thumb," in *The Panda's Thumb* (New York: W. W. Norton, 1980), 20.

18. Steve Jones, *Darwin's Ghost* (New York: Random House, 2000), 130–31.

19. Michael Ruse, *Darwinism Defended* (Reading, MA: Addison-Wesley, 1982), 40.

20. Edward O. Dodson and Peter Dodson, *Evolution: Process and Product*, 2nd ed. (New York: D. Van Nostrand, 1976), 29.

21. Niles Eldredge, *The Triumph of Evolution and the Failure of Creationism* (New York: W. H. Freeman, 2000), 146.

22. This section borrows from chap. 2 of Robert M. Burns, *The Great Debate on Miracles: From Joseph Glanvill to David Hume* (London: Associated University Press, 1981), 19.

23. Ibid., 20.

24. Ibid.

25. Ibid., 21–22.

26. Isaac Newton, *The Principia* (1687), translated by Andrew Motte (Amherst, NY: Prometheus, 1995), 442.

27. Burns, *Great Debate on Miracles*, 25.

28. Ibid., 26.

29. Ibid., 33.

30. For additional discussion see David Snokes, "The Problem of the Absolute in Evidential Epistemology," *Perspectives on Science and Christian Faith* 47 (1995).

31. Emphasis added; see Charles Darwin, *On the Origin of Species*, 6th ed. (1872; reprint London: Collier Macmillan, 1962), 182.

Index

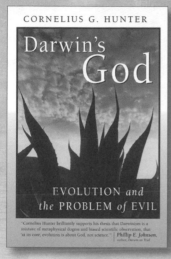
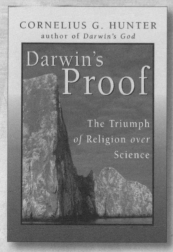